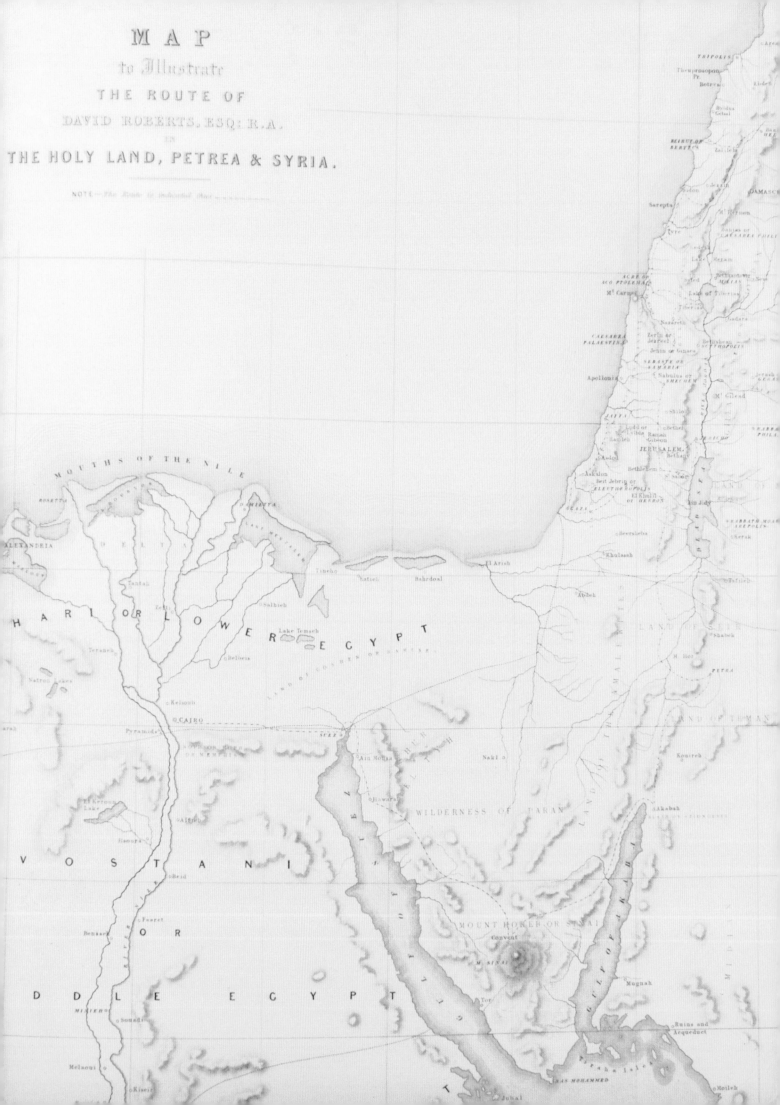

MAP
to Illustrate
THE ROUTE OF
DAVID ROBERTS, ESQ: R.A.
THE HOLY LAND, PETREA & SYRIA.

GOD'S COOKBOOK

GOD'S COOKBOOK

TRACING THE CULINARY TRADITIONS OF THE LEVANT

by Jamie d'Antioc

ARCADIAN LIFESTYLE

Designed and typeset by Phil Cleaver of etal-design consultants, Oxford & London
Photography by John Stone
Printed in the United Kingdom by Butler Tanner & Dennis, on Munken Lynx, free from chlorine (TCF)
and OBA and resistant to ageing in accordance with ISO 97006
Typeset in Monotype Arcadian Bembo

CONTENTS

Prologue 11

Introduction 15

Herbs, spices and other flavours 29

Bread 51

Dairy 71

Simple & side dishes 83

Soups & stews 131

Grain 155

Vegetables 177

Fish 203

Poultry 235

Meat 265

Desserts 297

Beverages 323

Inspired eating 335
Fasting, Digestion, Cleanliness, Prayer, Moderation, Vegetarianism, Feasting, Quick dishes suitable for children, Hunting

Index 359

ACKNOWLEDGEMENTS

I would like to acknowledge the invaluable contribution of all my research team, especially Jemima de Miéville, Deirdre Noonan, Liam, Rouena and Reine d'Antioc. Wada d'Antioc made a substantial contribution to recipe research and its application. Even though over thirty people were involved in recipe testing, William, the full-time family cook, should be singled out for his outstanding efforts. I must also extend my thanks to Mary, Brigitte, Diane and Sara-Rosa who helped with both testing and proof-reading, and provided invaluable moral support. Roy and Romain d'Antioc have made an important contribution towards the structure of the chapters, aided in no small way by Jem-Oli and Daisy. Jimmy, Lily, Reid, Remy and Romana helped with choosing and organising the layout of the illustrations. I must also thank Sana for her choice of quotations, as well as Alex Warren, Victoria Hanson, Daniel Hudspith and Jago Tennant for editing and proof-reading.

I thank my mother for her marvellous choice of illustrations from the family archives, whilst not the least of my gratitude must go to the ever-patient Phil Cleaver for solving the intricate jigsaw puzzle of our remarkable book design and to John Stone for the photography.

Jamie d'Antioc
Geneva, Switzerland

FOR MY GRANDMOTHER

*On her
one hundred and eighth
birthday*

'Blessed are those who hunger and thirst for righteousness,
for they shall be satisfied.'

MATTHEW 5:6

PROLOGUE

During the course of my life I have been lucky enough to have experienced the great diversity of peoples and cultures on this planet: from the Arabian Peninsula to Europe, the Holy Land to Africa, the Far East to the Americas. Although my experience is wide and varied, it is by no means complete – there are many places I have yet to visit and even more things to understand.

Through these experiences, however, I have learnt that even across such a variety of cultures and peoples certain bonds exist which inextricably link us all together: universal themes, hopes and basic needs that defy borders, politics and preconceptions. It is exactly these bonds that make us who we are at the most fundamental level, uniting us in the broadest of spectrums, within the realm of God.

It is distressing that in these days of conflict and chaos, rhetoric seems to encourage us to dwell on the differences between various religions. Christians, Jews and Muslims fight over details and particulars of worship and it appears to have been almost forgotten that the underlying belief of these three religions is synonymous: belief in one Almighty God and in His love for mankind.

This book does not aim to preach or dwell on human differences but to celebrate similarities and shared spiritual roots. It is intended as an appreciation of the oneness of the three Abrahamic faiths through the medium of the most universal preoccupation since the dawn of time: food. At the same time, this work is difficult to categorise, encompassing not only cookery but also art, religion and philosophy.

At the grand old age of one hundred and eight, my grandmother fell down and broke her hip. She had all her front teeth, creamy unwrinkled skin and lived every day to its full. I remember watching her morning ritual where she would recite her own poetry while massaging her hands and feet. She would feed us pistachios in July, walnuts in October and let us feast on fresh cream and honey all year round.

Having never been to visit a doctor in her life she refused to start at one hundred and eight. She was determined to live her life the way she always had and decided that her hip would heal by itself. She reminded me how Abraham, the father of the three faiths, had lived until the age of one hundred and seventy-five. He had spent most of his life wandering as a nomad, eating a diet of vegetables, fruit and honey and limiting his intake of meat to under one pound a week. Legend has it that, in the Land of the Fertile Crescent, he came upon a place where he found magnificent herds of cattle. The patriarch's fondness for cattle led him to settle in this corner of Northern Mesopotamia and call it 'Alep'. The origin of the Aramaic and Arabic words for milk, this place is known today as Aleppo.

My grandmother died in her bed happy and at peace. She never did go to see a doctor about her hip. The fact that she and several other members of my family have lived to over a hundred years of age led me to examine their diet. I discovered that their particular way of eating, which combines Levantine cuisine with a holistic approach to food, reflects many modern health plans and dietary 'revelations'. My grandmother insisted that food, faith, health and therefore longevity were all closely interrelated. Yet she never abandoned the basic principle that food was there to be enjoyed. This book recaptures the delicious and healthy recipes of my grandmother and tries to link them with an understanding of the food we have eaten throughout history, the foods sent to us by God. The remarkable beauty of the illustrations, which depict nature itself, remind us that God gave us these foods not only as physical and spiritual fuel, but as something to be enjoyed and appreciated.

INTRODUCTION

*'For the righteous shall be a blessed retreat;
the Gardens of Eden.
Reclining there with bashful virgins
for companions they will call for
abundant fruit and drink.'*

QURAN, SAD 38:48

THE PHILOSOPHY BEHIND THIS BOOK

Abraham, Jesus and Muhammad, the founders of the world's three principal mono-theistic faiths, all described heaven in a similar way: a wonderful place devoid of all worldly discomfort and toil, where everybody's needs are anticipated and love reigns supreme. The righteous inherit a lush paradise, the watered orchards of the gardens of Eden are restored and no one goes hungry.

In contrast, life on earth is driven by human subsistence, primarily the need for food. Since its earliest days, human history has always been dominated by the quest for food. It is a driving force at the very core of our existence and has shaped every aspect of our behaviour. In the search for the fuel that powers the human body, people have been motivated to learn about their environment and adapt accordingly over time. Having acquired a certain amount of knowledge we have learned the best ways to harness nature's resources, developing more and more efficient hunting tools, learning about the medicinal properties of plants, mastering animal and plant domestication, but most importantly by living according to necessity.

In the plenty of the modern world many of the principles by which our ancestors lived for thousands of years have been forgotten. Although understanding and respect for nature does exist in some of the more traditional communities, circumstances and attitudes concerning food and medicine in the West have changed so much over the last few centuries that these principles seem to have been all but abandoned.

To a certain extent, Western civilisation is dissociated from the natural world. The struggle for food has been replaced by the quest for wealth and power, together with a disregard for nature that many believe could lead to the destruction of the planet. Man has nearly forgotten that he himself is an animal, a part of nature, and it is only in nature itself that he can find sustenance. Dramatic changes in farming and food processing, particularly during the twentieth century, as well as the increased pace of modern life have dramatically altered our diet from that of our ancestors. Intensive farming has compromised the quality of life of our animals and consequently the quality of our food. Processed foods loaded with artificial sweeteners, flavourings and preservatives eaten in a 'grab and run' manner are destroying our physical and indeed mental and spiritual health. In these days of the McInstant, there is a general health and dietary malaise in the West. Enormous portions of foods that are high in carbohydrates and fat and low in vitamins, minerals and fibre, combined with stress and lack of exercise, are helping to hasten our dietary demise. Consequently, diet-related illnesses such as heart attacks and clinical obesity have become common problems.

It is only in recent years that people have seriously begun to question our dietary habits. Medicine is turning more and more to an examination of the foods we eat as it recognizes the preventive potential of a healthy diet. With an explosion in research into the phyto-chemicals, vitamins and minerals contained in plants and animal produce, the healing powers of certain foods are being rediscovered. Hippocrates' concept of letting our food be our medicine and medicine our food seems increasingly relevant. Naturally, of course, a good diet is only one of the requirements for good health and is greatly helped by exercise and relaxation. However, it is a good starting point.

Between protein powders and low-carb diets there are so many food fads and fashions today that is difficult to know where to begin to change the way we eat. Two key ideas can help to narrow our search: first is Herodotus' notion that the climate and topography of a land, and therefore the food it grows, moulds the character of its people. The second is the idea that nutritious and balanced food and drink produce character, and sound characters can often become respected and influential leaders. These ideas lead us straight to the Holy Land. After all, surely it is no coincidence that the three major monotheistic faiths, and their figureheads, all originated from the same area of the world? The region's three great spiritual leaders emerged in the Near East, the lands bordering Mesopotamia. It was over ten thousand years ago in this region, commonly known as the cradle of civilization (in and around the Khabur basin – modern-day Syria) that farming began.

Three great men of this region, Abraham, Jesus and Muhammad, all led similar lives, ate similar foods and lived according to the same abstemious, pious principles, guided by God. In terms of faith they have set an example for millions of people all over the world. Why then do we not follow their lifestyle guidelines as well? Should we not look to the environment, way of life and rules that nurtured the development of these great men, and indeed of our civilization, in order to understand our own minds, bodies and surroundings?

Throughout the Hebrew Scriptures, the New Testament, the Quran and the Hadith (the recorded sayings and acts of Muhammad) we are given pointers to the kinds of foods we should eat, as well as how and when to eat them, in order to live life to the fullest. More than simply recommending certain foods, these sources encourage us to exercise, to combine certain favourable foods and regulate our intake of others, all principles increasingly advocated by modern research into healthier living. The foods and recipes in God's Cookbook endeavour to follow this spiritual counsel. Where these pointers become unclear, history, archaeology and botany have been employed to put together a picture of the lifestyle of the people of the ancient Holy Land. God's Cookbook aims to respect their dietary guidelines, in however general a sense. Any foods that are prohibited by one or more of the three faiths have been omitted from this book and all recipes are designed to allow the reader to follow the dietary regulations of all three.

Perhaps, therefore, in our search for answers we should listen to God's views on food and lifestyle before looking elsewhere. After all, it is thanks to God that nature provides us so abundantly with all that we could want for a healthy and happy lifestyle, and it is mainly down to our own misuse of the raw materials given to us that pain, suffering and famine ensue. So, through examining the words of His prophets and messengers, let us be guided towards a healthier lifestyle; one shaped by God.

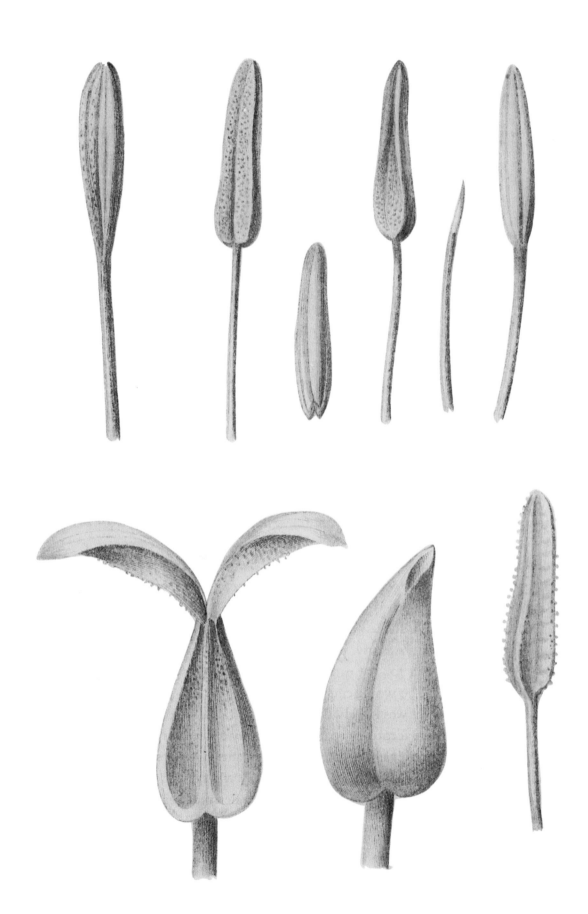

THE NEAR EAST – CRADLE OF CIVILIZATION

The annals of the first five books of the Old Testament, known as the Pentateuch, make up the common heritage of the three faiths of Judaism, Christianity and Islam. These faiths are often referred to as the 'Abrahamic religions', as they all have Abraham, father of many nations, as their patriarch. Although the chronicles of Moses and the Exodus, as well as Noah and the Ark, make up the common thread that links them, they have often been interpreted differently. Despite these differences, all three belief systems developed in and around the Fertile Crescent of the Near East within a period of about two and a half millennia.

Abraham is believed to have lived around 1800 BC according to the Gregorian calendar. The age of Abraham was that of the first dynasty of Babylon, whose most famous king was the Amorite codifier of laws, Hammurabi. Although born into polytheist Babylonian civilization, Abraham chose to live as a nomad, wandering around the plains of Mesopotamia in the service of his God. Although we have little historical evidence of his life, it seems that he made his way to Canaan with the community of which he was patriarch. During his long life, reputed to have been 175 years, he wandered as far south as Egypt and then throughout the Levant. The Pentateuch and the Quran both recount the stories of Abraham and his ancestors and descendants. Following the exodus from Egypt, the Hebrews settled in the Levant and wove the fabric of their civilization. As the structures of Judaism emerged, so too did the culinary traditions of the people. The Pentateuch was put in writing around 800 BC and numerous other Hebrew scriptures were composed in the centuries that followed. Although many people thought they had been delivered, life was harsh for the early Jews. Prophecies spoke of a Messiah, sent by God, who would end their suffering.

The early Hebrew diet was largely dependent on grains, vegetables and dairy products. They ate according to the topography of the land in which they lived. At that time the fertile Levant was abundant with vines, palms, pomegranates, olives and many other plants. Barley was the initial staple grain but was gradually supplanted by wheat. They derived their protein from pulses such as lentils and beans, as well as dairy products, particularly cheese and yogurt. The period of enslavement in Egypt influenced the culinary development of the Hebrews; the Bible recounts how the Jews lamented the foods they ate in Egypt while they were in the wilderness. Indeed it was during their wanderings that the manna and quails were sent down. Meat was rarely eaten, except during festivities when a lamb or goat was slaughtered. Dietary laws, which were laid down by Moses, became part of the culinary traditions of the Holy Land. Ritualistic slaughter practices emerged, pork and other 'unclean foods' were prohibited and the mixing of dairy produce and meat was avoided. The culinary identity of the nation of Israel was established; lamb and bitter herbs were eaten to commemorate the Passover.

The birth of Jesus of Nazareth is commonly estimated at 6 BC. He was born in the classical age when the Roman Empire controlled the whole Mediterranean. The Hebrew power base was unsteady and the Eastern province of Palestine was ruled by figureheads, the Herods. Born in Bethlehem, Jesus was raised in Nazareth and only began to travel at the age of thirty, when he proceeded to the Galilee region after his sojourn in the desert. It seems that he also went to Tyre, Sidon and, towards the end of his life, Jerusalem. Following his execution by the Romans, his disciples recorded his life and teachings in what later became the New Testament of the Bible. In the centuries that followed his death, the Emperor Constantine was converted and Christianity took hold as the principal religion in the Near East. After the quelling of a revolt in 70 AD, the Jewish population of Palestine diminished as they were expelled by the Romans or left to find another way of life.

At the time of Jesus of Nazareth, the strongest culinary influences in the Levant came from the classical world. As a consequence of the campaigns of Alexander the Great, new foods, such as rice, which became the preferred grain of the urban elite, were introduced in the Levant. The Romans also introduced several new foods to the region, including chickens, which fast became the most popular fowl. The sophistication of Roman cuisine can be seen in the first-century work entitled 'The Books of Apicius', which contain a plethora of recipes which employ varied ingredients and cooking methods. The classical style of dining, where guests lay on couches, using limited utensils to cut food into bite-sized portions, was adopted in affluent Levantine homes.

By the birth of Muhammad, estimated at 570 AD, Christianity had become the principal religion in the Levant. The region was then part of the Eastern Roman or Byzantine Empire, which was ruled from Constantinople. The prophet was born in Mecca, a Hijaz city characterised by idolatry and polytheism, yet he came into contact with a considerable number of Jews and Christians in his youth. From 610 AD until his death in 632 AD, he recited the message he received from God through the angel Gabriel. This recital is known as the Quran. Following his death his disciples assembled the Quran into one coherent text. Furthermore, they and those around him recorded his sayings and told stories of his life. The sayings and acts of Muhammad are collectively known as the Hadith. A military campaign which would result in the far-reaching spread of Islam had begun before Muhammad's death. The conquest of the Levant was completed under the reign of the caliph Omar I, Damascus falling in 635 AD and Sophronius, the Patriarch of Jerusalem, surrendering in 637 AD. In less than a century Islam took hold as the principal religion of the Holy Land, although Jewish and Christian populations still existed. The centuries following the death of Muhammad saw Arabic become the language of the Mediterranean, and a period of cultural excellence ensued.

The advent of Islam and the conquest of the Mediterranean region by the Arabs brought about a shift in Levantine cuisine. Primarily, Muslims were instructed to follow the dietary law set down by Muhammad. Animals were ritually slaughtered in the name of Allah, blood was drained from meat and swine became prohibited. The unifying effect of an empire that stretched from Central Asia to Spain also permeated cuisine, the influence of Persian cooking having a particularly prominent effect. Vegetables such as the aubergine became commonplace all over the Arab empire including the Levant, whilst culinary excellence was pursued under the Bagdahd caliphates. By the thirteenth century, a cookbook known as *Kitab al Tabikh,* or 'A Baghdad Cookery book', had been compiled comprising of the recipes of the preceding centuries.

COOKING METHODS

The earliest cooking was done over an open fire. An earthenware or metal vessel was placed on the fire and the food was cooked slowly, generally boiled or braised. Food could also be fried in this way, depending on the availability of fats and oils. The development of cooking methods, in particular the oven, greatly changed cuisine. The most primitive ovens consisted of a simple cavity dug out in the floor of a tent, house or courtyard. These cavities were then lined with clay and filled with embers. In the early Hebrew period they were often fuelled with dung, but wood fires later became the standard as populations settled. As time went on, ovens were made entirely from clay, either free-standing or built against a wall. Sophisticated beehive-shaped ovens, which frequently served a whole village, were used by bakers to make breads. A tightly sealed earthenware container was often buried in embers, or placed in a clay oven, and the dish left to cook slowly. The food itself would commonly be encased in clay, salt or dough and cooked in a similar manner. Meats were typically marinated and cooked over an open fire or on skewers over the embers of a pit oven, quite similar to a barbecue.

AT THE ANCIENT TABLE

Most people in the ancient Levant ate only two meals a day. The first took place in the late morning and typically consisted of bread dipped in olive oil or vinegar, toasted wheat, olives, figs or some other vegetables or fruit. This meal would have often been a break from work and usually eaten under the shade of a tree. The main meal of the day was served just before sunset. People gathered around a stove or an open fire and ate communally from a large pot, while in wealthier houses they sat on cushions or low stools. This meal usually comprised a soup or potage of seasoned vegetables and pulses into which bread was dipped. Meat and fowl were only consumed by the very wealthy on a regular basis and were rarely available to the common people, except on certain feast days. Fish was more readily obtainable. The Roman *cena* was adopted by the Levantine elite during the classical period as later the sophisticated culinary habits of the Baghdadi caliphates were copied in the early Islamic times. Few utensils, such as knives and forks, were used in the ancient Levant. The Romans had spoons, with which they used to cook and eat, yet it is unlikely that they were used in the Levant, where bread was used to mop up soups and potages. Later, food was often cut up into small pieces before it was served and eaten with hands or made into parcels with bread or salad leaves.

A NOTE ON THE SPIRITUAL TEXTS

Quotes from the Hebrew scriptures, commonly known as the Old Testament of the Holy Bible, are referred to by book, chapter and verse number, e.g. GENESIS I:I

Quotes from the life and teachings of Jesus of Nazareth, commonly known as the New Testament of the Holy Bible, are referred to by book, chapter and verse number, e.g. MATTHEW I:I

The Holy Quran. This is referred to as Quran, and by book, book number and surah or verse number, e.g. QURAN, THE EXORDIUM I:I

The Hadith is the recorded sayings and acts of the prophet Muhammad. It supplements the Quran as a source of Islamic religious law. Sayings and life of Muhammad are referenced as being related by AL BUKHARI or related by a third party and recorded in AL BUKHARI.

'The Medicine of the Prophet' by Jalalu'd-Din Abd'ur-Rahman As Suyuti is a book of medicine based on the Quran and the Hadith. Sayings and acts of Muhammad are referenced as being related by AS SUYUTI or related by another party and recorded in AS SUYUTI.

David Roberts. R.A.

HERBS, SPICES

AND OTHER FLAVOURS

'But woe unto you, Pharisees!
For ye tithe mint and rue and all manner
of herbs, and pass over judgement
and the love of God.'

LUKE 11:42

HERBS, SPICES
AND OTHER FLAVOURS

Herbs and spices rarely comprise the main ingredient in any dish, yet they have been invaluable in cuisine since ancient times. A good cook's employment of these two essentials can lift the blandest of dishes. Holy Land cooks relied heavily on herbs and spices to add flavour to the monotony of the many soups and potages, often based on legumes, which made up the main part of their diet. Particular uses of herbs are interesting as they evolve according to geographical and cultural factors, whilst flavours come to be associated with regions, communities and families. Herbs and spices were highly prized for their varied and distinctive aromas in ancient times. Frequent reference is made to them throughout the Old Testament, the New Testament, the Quran and the Hadith. Most notable are the 'bitter herbs' of the Old Testament, which have become an important part of traditional Jewish Passover festivities. Many important herbs of the region, such as parsley, are not specifically named in the spiritual texts. Instead there are repeated general references to 'herbs'. Similarly, in the early Islamic cookery book known as *Kitab al Tabikh*, the reader is frequently told to use 'the usual herbs and spices'. Herbs and spices were employed in numerous ways; habitually they were used to season salads and raw vegetables as well as to flavour cooked dishes. At Holy Land tables, bread was dipped in oil and then in a blend of ground spices. Many households had their own signature blend of spices, which was served with every meal. Herbal infusions were brewed for various medicinal purposes, such as mint which soothed the digestive system, or simply for their aroma. Mint leaves were scattered on floors of ancient synagogues and thyme was burned in the classical world for its fragrance. For the recipes in this book fresh herbs and spices are frequently employed, and can be prepared using a pestle and mortar or a modern spice grinder. Seasonally available herbs, such as mint, can also be dried out to last through the winter.

PARADISE DRY SPICE MIX

1 nutmeg
2 teaspoons black pepper
2 teaspoons cloves
2 cinnamon sticks
3cm (1 in) ginger
1 teaspoon salt
1 teaspoon white pepper or cumin

Grind the spices in a pestle and mortar
or a spice grinder. The mix can be
stored in a glass airtight jar. This mix is
ideal for seasoning meat and should be
rubbed on a cut or joint 1 hour prior
to cooking.

PARADISE GREEN HERBS

4 tablespoons parsley, finely chopped
2 tablespoons tarragon, finely
chopped
4 tablespoons thyme, finely chopped
4 tablespoons rosemary,
finely chopped
1 teaspoon salt

Combine the herbs, salt and spices.
Use to season meat and vegetables
within three days.

SALT

'You are the salt of the earth.' MATTHEW 5:13

Jesus likened the multitudes to the salt of the earth. Due to its high sodium content, salt is essential to life. The position of salt in the history of humankind reflects this fact; the English word salary is derived from the Latin term for salt, whilst during the reign of Antiochus Epiphanes Levantine salt was even taxed by the Syrians to pay the Romans. As early as Leviticus the importance of salt, the symbol of God's covenant with his people, was established by Moses. *'You shall not omit salt from your grain offerings of your covenant with God. With all your offerings you shall offer salt.'* (LEVITICUS 2:13). Along the coast, large pans were filled with sea water and left to evaporate in the heat of the sun. However, it was also mined in the salt pits of the Dead Sea. Sea salt is considered to have the most delicate flavour, yet the mined rock variety is more suitable to some dishes, especially those actually baked in salt. In addition to seasoning, salting was the principal method of preserving food in the ancient world.

PEPPER

Pepper, or *piper nigrum*, which strictly speaking is simply black pepper, has been cultivated in India for over 3000 years. It was still uncommon in the Levant at the time of Jesus, where cumin provided the 'hot' taste in cooking. However, it was known in Egypt and the classical world, where its high price was lamented by Pliny. Pepper was widely available during the early Islamic period and is mentioned by As Suyuti as having carminative properties. In the centuries following The Crusades it became one of the most sought-after spices in medieval Europe.

ANTIOCH TABLE SPICE

3 tablespoons thyme
1 tablespoon chickpea flour
3 tablespoons sumac
1 tablespoon coriander seeds, toasted
1 tablespoon whole wheat, toasted
3 tablespoons sesame seeds, toasted
1 tablespoon nutmeg, ground
1 tablespoon salt

Toast coriander seeds, whole wheat
and sesame seeds separately. Then
place in a pestle and mortar or a spice
grinder and lightly grind. Mix in the
remaining ingredients and transfer to a
tight-fitting glass jar to store. Guests
can dip their bread in olive oil and
then the spice mix.

OLIVE

'It is He who sends down water from the sky, which provides you with your drink and brings forth pasturage on which your cattle feed. And with it He brings forth corn and olives, dates and grapes and fruits of every kind. Surely in this there is a sign for thinking men.' QURAN, CATTLE 6:141

I t would be difficult to exaggerate the importance of the olive in the ancient world. Although it is mentioned less frequently than the fig or the vine, the olive stands out as the Biblical tree *par excellence*. In classical mythology, the goddess Athena was credited with giving the olive plant to mankind. Its name, however, *Olea europaea*, is misleading as the olive originates in Western Asia and not Europe. Originally the olive grew wild in the Near East; it was an olive branch that the dove brought Noah to symbolize the end of the flood. Archaeological evidence suggests that the olive plant was domesticated in the eastern Mediterranean as long as ten thousand years ago. The Levant fast became renowned for its olive groves, to the extent that Moses called Palestine a 'land of olive oil'. Both the young green and the ripened black fruits of the olive tree were enjoyed in antiquity after their bitter juices were extracted through treatment. Yet the olive gained its prominence primarily through its oil, which was highly symbolic. It was used to anoint in sanctification and consecration ceremonies. Olive oil is still used to anoint priests in the Roman Catholic and Orthodox churches today. This thick, nutritious oil can help to lower both blood pressure and cholesterol, whilst also serving as a tonic for hair and skin. Furthermore, the antibacterial and medicinal properties of the olive meant that it could be used in surgical operations without risk. As Suyuti claimed that olive oil delayed old age and wrote that the prophet Muhammad went as far as calling olives 'the medicine of the poor'. The whole fruit, including the pit, was pressed to extract an inferior oil which was burned in lamps. Extra virgin and virgin olive oil, which are produced from the first and second pressings of the fruit respectively, are known to have the lowest acidity and the best flavour. They are therefore the preferred oils used to season salads and vegetables.

CITRUS FRUIT

'The citrus fruit is like a true believer, with a good taste, and a good scent.' SAYING OF MUHAMMAD RELATED BY AL BUKHARI

The citrus fruit family probably evolved in South or South-East Asia about 8000 years ago. During the captivity in Babylon the Hebrews became familiar with the citron, the now virtually extinct ancestor of the more palatable lemon and orange. They brought *Citrus medica* or *etrog* as it was known in Hebrew with them on their return to the Holy Land, where it came to play an important part in the Feast of the Tabernacles synagogue service. During the later classical period, Jewish farmers are said to have grafted the lemon from the citron. After the Jewish rebellion of 66–70 AD, the Hebrews were dispersed throughout the Roman Empire and spread citrus fruit around the Mediterranean. By the early Islamic period, lemons and oranges, known as sweet citron, had become common-place at Levantine tables. As Suyuti recounts how Ayesha, a wife of Muhammad, gave lemon wedges dipped in honey to a blind man visiting her tent. Citrus fruits are an excellent source of vitamin C. As Suyuti said that eating lemons could diminish sorrow and desolation of the self, whilst oranges fortified the heart.

CITRUS DRESSING

60 ml (4 tablespoons) lemon juice
60 ml (4 tablespoons) olive oil
Salt and pepper

Combine the lemon juice, oil, salt and pepper. For a low-fat alternative simply dress salads or vegetables with lemon juice and season.

VINEGAR

'At mealtime Boaz said to her, "Come here, and eat some of this bread, and dip your morsel in the sour wine." So she sat beside the reapers and he heaped up for her parched grain. She ate until she was satisfied, and she had some left over.' RUTH 2:14

Vinegar was widely enjoyed in ancient times. Wine vinegar, diluted with water, was a popular beverage in ancient Palestine [NUMBERS 6:3; RUTH 2:14]. Although it was often administered as a punishment, it is possible that the offer of the 'gall' filled sponge to Jesus during the crucifixion was simply an act of kindness. Vinegar was called 'a comfort for man' by Muhammad, was said to aid digestion and according to As Suyuti can even act as a mild painkiller. It is an important seasoning in many vegetable and salad dishes, as well as an essential ingredient in pickling. Vinegar, which is essentially acetic acid, can be made from a variety of products and is often infused with various fruits and herbs. It should be noted that some vinegar with a high alcohol content does not comply with Muslim dietary law.

VINAIGRETTE

15 ml (1 tablespoon) vinegar
½ teaspoon mustard
5ml (1 teaspoon) water
90ml (6 tablespoons) olive oil
2 tablespoons shallots or fresh herbs such as tarragon, basil, parsley or marjoram, finely chopped
Salt and pepper

Combine the mustard, vinegar and water. Season with salt and pepper, then slowly whisk in the oil. Mix in the shallots or herbs. Serve with green salad or vegetables.

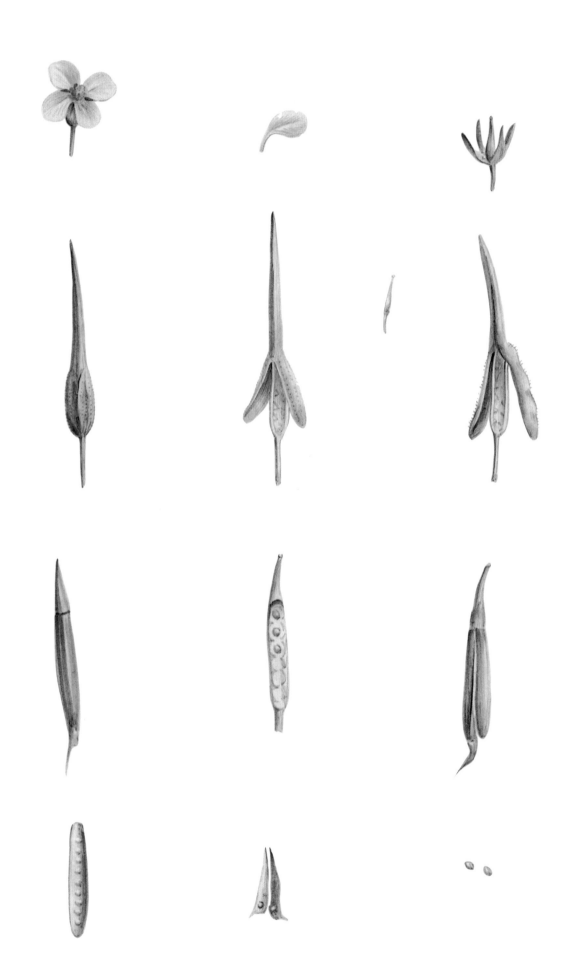

MUSTARD

HERBS, SPICES AND OTHER FLAVOURS

'The kingdom of heaven is like a mustard seed that someone took and sowed in his field: it is the smallest of all seeds, but when it has grown, it is the greatest of shrubs.'
MATTHEW 13:31

These tiny, pungent seeds are produced from the mustard plant, a member of the cabbage family. They grew wild along the Plain of Gennesaret, where Jesus taught the multitudes. Mustard seeds are referred to throughout both the Bible and the Quran, although scholars disagree as to whether these references are to the common black mustard seed, *Brassica nigra,* or the white mustard seed *Sinapis alba.* The small mustard seeds are particularly noted for their ability to grow into enormous plants, some growing as high as fifteen feet and as thick as a man's arm. As a result, they are often used as a metaphor to explain the concepts of faith and membership of organized religion to children. Mustard is most valued for its spicy flavour; when crushed the oily seeds form a paste, which makes a tasty accompaniment to food, particularly meat dishes. Its seeds are known to have antibacterial and decongestant properties.

'We shall set up the scales on the day of Resurrection, so that no man in the least shall be wronged. Actions as small as a grain of mustard seed shall be weighed out. Our reckoning shall suffice.' QURAN, THE PROPHETS 21:40

MUSTARD AND HONEY DRESSING

15g (1 tablespoon) whole grain mustard
15g (1 tablespoon) honey
45ml (3 tablespoons) lemon juice
45ml (3 tablespoons) olive oil
Salt and pepper

Combine the mustard, honey and lemon juice, season with salt and pepper and then the oil. Serve with green salad.

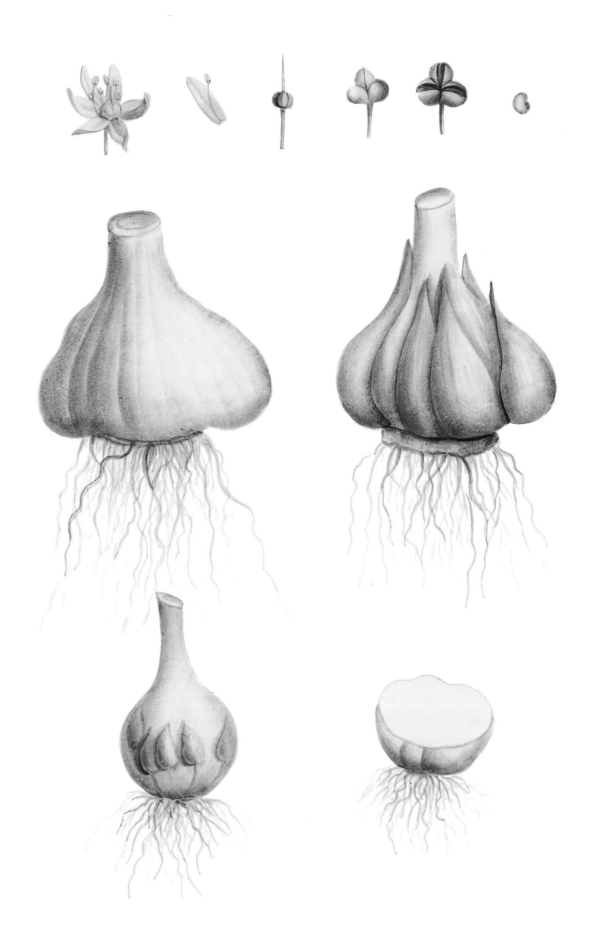

GARLIC

'People who have eaten garlic should keep clear of our mosques!' SAYING OF MUHAMMAD RELATED BY AL BURKHARI

Legend in Turkey and the Orient has it that when Satan stepped out of the garden of Eden after the 'fall' of mankind, onions sprang from where he placed his right foot and garlic from where he placed his left. Garlic's strong odour has been controversial throughout history. Muhammad's extreme dislike of the vegetable's smell was mirrored by aristocrats in ancient Rome. Yet its healing properties and health benefits have meant that garlic was also considered to have magical properties, being sacred, for instance, to the ancient Egyptians. Clay models of the bulb were even found in Tutankhamun's tomb. Cultivated garlic, or *Allium sativum*, probably originated from wild garlic (*Allium longicuspis*) in Central Asia. It is known to have been cultivated in Egypt and Mesopotamia as early as 2000 BC.

This pungent culinary stimulant has a long history as a healing and strengthening food. It was so popular with the Hebrews that it was one of the foods they lamented leaving behind in Egypt. The perennial bulb is renowned for its anti-bacterial, anti-fungal and anti-thrombotic qualities. Hippocrates believed that garlic vapours could also be used to help treat cervical cancer. Even Muhammad, although he did not personally like the smell, appreciated the vegetable's benefits and encouraged people to eat it with the instruction, *'O ʿAli, eat garlic, were it not for my being visited by the angel of Allah (Jibril), I would eat it myself'* [SAYING OF MUHAMMAD RELATED IN AS-SUYUTI]. As a general rule the odour of garlic is significantly reduced when eaten with parsley or when cooked, especially boiled. Garlic presses allow the modern cook to avoid touching the cloves directly.

Modern research indicates that age-old fascination with garlic was entirely justified; it is so packed with healing, medicinal qualities as to be virtually a wonder food. Although nowadays garlic is most renowned for being beneficial to the heart, it has also been shown to inhibit platelet aggression. The bulb has many other attributes besides: diuretic, antioxidant, anti-inflammatory and carminative. It has even been found to have anti-carcinogenic properties, particularly related to gastric and colon cancers. Furthermore, garlic can be used as a mild painkiller or sedative and has antiviral and antibiotic qualities. In addition, the bulb is a good source of vitamins B1 and C.

GARLIC DRESSING

Half a garlic clove, finely minced
5ml (1 teaspoon) white wine vinegar
15ml (1 tablespoon) lemon juice
½ teaspoon mustard
60ml (4 tablespoons) olive oil
Salt and pepper

Mix the garlic, vinegar, lemon juice and mustard together. Season with salt and pepper and slowly whisk in the oil.

GARLIC AND ALMOND SAUCE

1 garlic clove
60ml (4 tablespoons) white wine vinegar
125g (4 ounces) white bread, with crusts removed
110g (½ cup) ground almonds
125ml (½ cup) olive oil
Salt and pepper

1. Peel and halve the clove. Leave to soak in the vinegar for 5 minutes. Remove the cloves and reduce to a pulp using a pestle and mortar. Season with salt and pepper.
2. Soak the bread in water for 2 minutes, remove and squeeze off any excess water. Combine the bread and garlic and mix in the remaining vinegar.
3. Beat in the almonds, olive oil, lemon juice and season with salt and pepper. Serve cold with fish or vegetables.

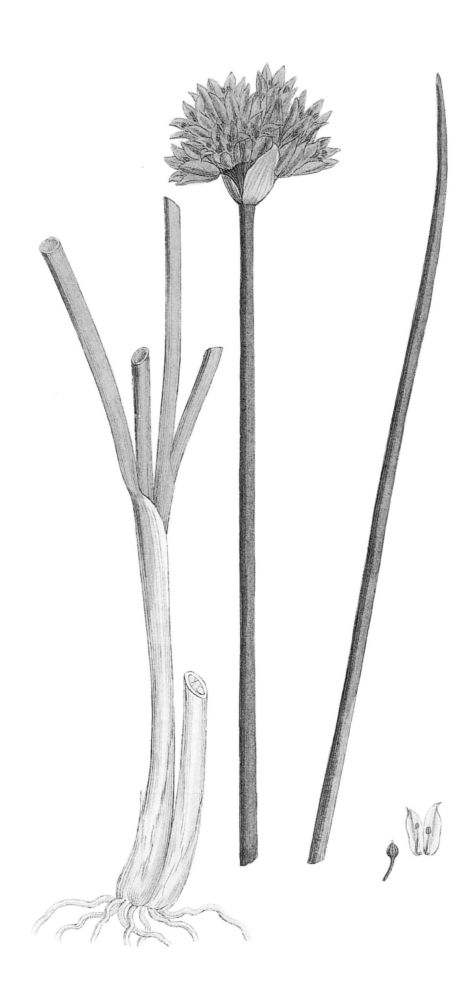

BREAD

'I am the bread of life.
Your ancestors ate the manna in the
wilderness, and they died.
This is the bread that comes down
from heaven so that one may
eat of it and not die.'

JOHN 6:48–51

BREAD

'Give us this day our daily bread.' LUKE 11:3

Bread stands out as the most significant of all foods mentioned in the spiritual texts. Often employed to represent food generically, it was considered a minimum for human existence in the ancient world. Legend has it that the angel Gabriel took pity on Adam after his expulsion from the Garden of Eden and showed him how to grind grains into flour to make bread: the first dish on earth. The most prominent staple of the Holy Land, it is the only food for which there is a recipe in the Old Testament. Unleavened bread is still eaten at the Jewish Passover to commemorate their hasty departure from Egypt. In the book of Leviticus it was prohibited to offer any type of bread, other than unleavened, to Yahweh. Indeed, bread was such a prominent staple that it is mentioned over thirty times throughout the Bible and its image is employed in many proverbs.

The employment of bread as a symbol in the New Testament reaches its zenith when Jesus is referred to as the bread of life. At the Last Supper, Jesus asked the apostles to break bread in His memory. Bread was served at almost every meal in the ancient Levant, where it was as much a utensil as a food. The wealthy ate refined wheat bread whereas the poor had to make do with darker breads made from grains such as barley, millet and rye. In times of hardship, bread was made out of practically anything that could be ground into flour, even acorns collected from the woods. Tenth-century physician and author of 'The Medicine of the Prophet', As Suyuti believed that soft bread was most nutritious and easily digested.

Physicians in the early Islamic period, and indeed in medieval Europe, recommended soft white bread for those who led a sedentary lifestyle and thought the darker, cruder loaves were best left to the labouring masses who exerted themselves sufficiently to digest them.

THE MILLSTONE

'No one shall take a mill or an upper millstone in pledge, for that would be taking a life in pledge.' DEUTERONOMY 24:6

Bread was baked on a daily basis in the Holy Land. As milled flour quickly turned rancid, grains were milled every day. The most basic domestic millstone would have comprised a fixed concave bottom stone and a mobile convex upper stone. The upper stone was turned by hand, but larger and more commercial models were operated by a slave or an animal. Every house had its own millstone, protected by mosaic law since the survival of a household fallen upon hard times depended on its ability to produce its own bread. Traditionally, it was the women of a household who were responsible for milling grain.

LEAVEN

'The kingdom of heaven is like yeast that a woman took and mixed in with three measures of flour until all of it was leavened.' MATTHEW 13:33

The Bible is peppered with references to raising agents. The permeation of dough by yeast is used as a metaphor to describe both the power of the kingdom of heaven and the threat of the influence of malice in the world. The word leaven refers to any form of raising agent used in bread and cakes. Since ancient times, this has most commonly been a piece of fermented dough from a previous batch of bread. Archaeological evidence suggests that the ancient Egyptians used saccaromycetes, a liquid extracted during the brewing of beer from 1500 BC onwards. Leavened bread and cakes were eaten but never offered to God. They were also prohibited on certain feast days such as the Passover.

BAKING

'He looked and there was at his head a cake baked on hot stones, and a jar of water. He ate and drank and lay down again.' I KINGS 19:6

One of the earliest methods of baking bread involved placing the dough on 'bake stones', which were put directly in the fire. Surprisingly, these fires were often fuelled by dung. Sarah, wife of Abraham, is the earliest baker mentioned in the Old Testament. She would have probably had a makeshift oven in her tent, a conical earthenware vessel over a fire. Life was harsh for the early Hebrews; their humble meals were a far cry from the elegant banquets of the Assyrian kings. Later, wood-fired beehive or igloo-shaped ovens were developed, in which bread was stuck to the walls or baked on purpose-built shelves. Traditionally, baking was a female occupation but as ovens developed it became more economical for towns to have a communal oven manned by a baker. Wood was brought to fire the bakers' ovens on donkeys and children brought their families loaves on stones or trays. It could take a whole day to heat up the ovens, which were thus left alight and often required supervision. There was even a baker street in Jerusalem: *'and a loaf of bread was given him daily from the baker's street, until all the bread of the city was gone'* [JEREMIAH 37:21]. As Suyuti thought that the best type of bread was made from fine flour and was baked in circular-shaped ovens.

'Honour bread, for Allah has made the earth and the sky its servants.'
SAYING OF MUHAMMAD BY AYESHA, RELATED IN AS SUYUTI

KHOUBIZ FLAT BREAD

840g (6 cups) white flour
1 sachet active dry yeast
500ml (2 cups) warm water
1 ½ teaspoons salt
1 teaspoon sugar
30ml (2 tablespoons) oil

1. Sift the flour into a large mixing bowl and warm gently in a low oven.
2. Dissolve the yeast in 60ml (½ cup) of warm water, add the remaining water and stir in the salt and sugar.
3. Set aside half of the flour. Pour the liquid into the remaining flour and stir until it becomes a thick viscous liquid. Cover with a cloth and leave in a warm place for 20 minutes when air bubbles should form.
4. Stir in the rest of the flour and gradually add the oil. Beat the mixture well until it becomes a soft dough.
5. Knead the dough on a floured board for about 10 minutes until it takes on a satin-like texture. Shape into a ball.
6. Roll the ball of dough in an oiled bowl, so that it is coated with oil on all sides. Cover and leave in a warm place for 1 to 2 hours by which time it should have doubled in size.

7. Pre-heat the oven to 250C (500F).
8. Transfer the dough back onto a floured board, knead lightly and divide into 8 pieces. Roll each piece into a thin disc. Cover with cloth and leave to stand for 15 minutes.
9. Heat a large, lightly-oiled baking sheet in the warmest part of the oven, bake the loaves separately for about 5 minutes each. Once they puff up, turn over, so that they are crisp on both sides. If serving immediately, wrap in a cloth to keep warm. Alternatively, reconstitute frozen loaves by spraying lightly with water and toasting until crisp.

SPELT

'And you take wheat and barley, beans and lentils, millet and spelt; put them into a vessel, and make bread for yourself. During the number of days that you lie on your side, three hundred and ninety days, you shall eat it.' EZEKIEL 4:9

A lthough spelt was certainly considered inferior to wheat in the Holy Land, it was preferred to barley as a crop for its ability to thrive in virtually any type of soil or conditions. Some versions of the Bible refer directly to 'spelt', whereas in others the word has been translated as 'rie' or 'rye'. In any case, it is generally agreed to be *Triticum spelta*, as mentions of 'rye' in the Bible actually refer to spelt, given that modern-day rye was unknown in the region in ancient times. Spelt is similar to wheat in appearance and taste, but has larger hulls. It can serve as an alternative to wheat for those allergic to gluten and even contains more protein, fat, fibre, B vitamins as well as complex carbohydrates, which are thought to stimulate the body's immune system. In recent years the macrobiotic and natural foods movements have brought spelt considerable popularity.

JERUSALEM SIEGE BREAD

The Lord instructed the prophet Ezekiel to make use of all the grains available to the people of Jerusalem, including less popular ones such as spelt, and make these loaves to see them through the Babylonian siege. This 'recipe' seemed to advise the people as to how to effectively manage their provisions. These protein-enriched loaves were made in haste with whatever grains and pulses were available.

2 tablespoons dry yeast
325ml (1 ¼ cups) warm water
560g (4 cups) white flour
70g (½ cup) barley flour
35g (¼ cup) spelt flour
35g (¼ cup) millet meal
35g (¼ cup) lentil meal
35g (¼ cup) chickpea meal
90ml (6 tablespoons) olive oil
2 teaspoons salt
30g (2 tablespoons) honey
2 tablespoons cumin seeds

'When they have levelled its surface ... do they not scatter dill, cumin and put wheat in rows and barley in its proper place, and spelt as the border? For they are well instructed; their God teaches them.' ISAIAH 28:25

1. Dissolve the yeast in a little of the water for 15–20 minutes so that it begins to froth.
2. Sieve the white flour into a mixing bowl and combine with the other dry ingredients.
3. Make a well in the centre of the mixture. Pour the yeast mixture and honey into the well. Mix together and gradually add in 4 tablespoons of the oil and the rest of the water.
4. Work the mixture by hand until it begins to resemble a soft dough. Transfer to a floured board and knead until the dough takes on a satin-like texture. Leave to rest for 5 minutes.
5. Divide the dough into 4 pieces, roll each piece into a ball and flatten into thin discs on a floured board. Leave in a warm place for 1 hour, after which they should have doubled in size.
6. Smear the loaves with the remaining oil and sprinkle with the cumin seeds. Place in a pre-heated oven at 200C (400F). Bake for 45 minutes.

WHOLE FLAT BREAD

280g (2 cups) wholemeal flour
170ml (⅔ cup) warm water
½ teaspoon salt
½ sachet dry yeast

1. Sieve the flour into a mixing bowl and combine with the salt. Dissolve yeast in a little water, then add the flour and mix into a soft dough. Transfer to a floured board and knead until it takes on a satin-like texture, roll into a ball.
2. Place in a lightly oiled bowl, cover and leave for 1 hour in a warm place to double in size.
3. Divide the dough into 8 pieces, roll each piece into a ball and flatten into thin discs on a floured board. Cover with a cloth and leave to rest for 30 minutes.
4. Place on a baking tray and bake for 30 minutes in an oven at 250C (500F).

UNLEAVENED BREAD

280g (2 cups) wholemeal flour
185ml (¾ cup) water
1 teaspoon sea salt
1 tablespoon toasted cumin seeds
Olive oil, to fry

1. Sieve the flour into a large mixing bowl and combine with the salt. Make a well in the centre of the flour and slowly pour in the water.
2. Mix until it begins to resemble a soft dough. Transfer to a floured board and knead until the dough takes on a satin-like texture.
3. Divide the dough into 4 pieces. Roll into balls and flatten into discs. Sprinkle each loaf with cumin seeds.
4. Cook 2 minutes on each side in an oiled and heated pan. Serve hot.

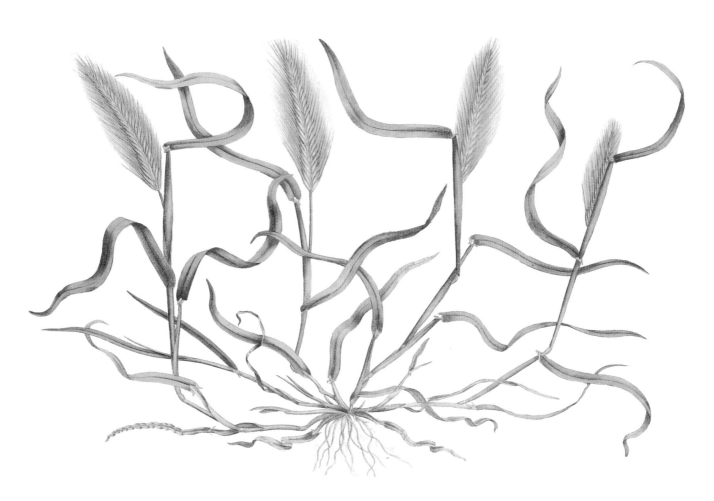

'For the Lord your God is bringing you into a good land, a land of brooks of water,
of fountains and springs, flowing forth in valleys and hills, a land of wheat and
barley, of vines and fig trees… in which you will eat bread without scarcity.'

DEUTERONOMY 8:7–9

BARLEY

'So they gathered them up, and from the fragments of the five barley loaves, left by those who had eaten, they filled twelve baskets.' JOHN 6:13

Although barley has never been considered the cream of crops, it was widely consumed in the ancient world. *Hordeum vulgare* seems to have been first cultivated in the fertile crescent about 8000 BC, its domestication running just parallel to, or perhaps even preceding, that of wheat. Archaeological evidence of domesticated six-row barley has been found in Syria and around the Sea of Galilee, where it was the food of the poor masses. While wheat was considered the more choice grain, barley is nutritionally rich and can be quite tasty. It was from five barley loaves that Jesus fed five thousand in the parable [JOHN 6:5–14]. It was ground to make a type of gruel or porridge and was baked into loaves alone or combined with other grains. As well as being affordable to the Holy Land poor, barley is an excellent source of soluble fibre, which research has shown to help reduce blood cholesterol and so fight coronary heart disease.

BARLEY LOAVES

½ sachet dry active yeast
85ml (⅓ cup) warm water
125ml (½ cup) yogurt
½ teaspoon bicarbonate of soda
70g (½ cup) barley flour
70g (½ cup) wholewheat flour
¼ teaspoon salt

1. Dissolve the yeast in warm water. Mix the yogurt with the bicarbonate of soda in a separate bowl until it froths.

2. Sift the flours into a mixing bowl with the salt. Gently pour in the liquid, then the yogurt and stir until it becomes dough-like. Work the mixture by hand until it begins to resemble a soft dough. Transfer to a floured board and knead until the dough takes on a satin-like texture.
3. Place in a lightly oiled bowl, cover and leave for 1 hour in a warm place to double in size.
4. Transfer back onto a floured board, divide into 8 pieces. Roll the balls out

to make a flat disc about 15cm
(6 inches) in diameter. Cover with
a cloth and leave to stand for
30 minutes.
5. Bake in a hot oven (250C, 500F) for
30 minutes.
6. Lightly oil the pan in between each
loaf. Cover the cooked loaves in a
cloth to keep them warm.

FATAH WITH CHICKPEAS
AND OLIVE OIL

4 flat bread loaves
450g (1 pound) chickpeas,
soaked overnight
125ml (½ cup) olive oil
2 garlic cloves
130g (1 cup) pine nuts
1 teaspoon cumin
Salt, to season

1. Drain the chickpeas and place them
in a saucepan of boiling water. Cook
for 1 hour and season with salt.
2. Chop the bread into bite-sized

pieces and lay out on a serving dish.
3. Pour 1 litre of the hot cooking
liquid over the pieces of bread and
leave to absorb. Lay the cooked
chick-peas on the soaked bread.
4. Fry the pine nuts and garlic until
browned. Scatter the nuts and drizzle
the pine nut and garlic-infused olive
oil on the dish. Season with cumin,
add salt as required and serve hot.

HUMMUS FATAH

4 flat bread loaves
450g (1 pound) chickpeas,
soaked overnight
Juice of 2 lemons
45g (3 tablespoons) sesame seed paste
130g (1 cup) pine nuts
15g (1 tablespoon) butter
Salt, to season
Parsley, to garnish

1. Drain the chick peas and place them
in a saucepan of boiling water. Cook
for 1 hour and season with salt.
2. Chop the bread into bite-size pieces

SOAKED FLAT BREADS

Flat bread can easily be reconstituted and was therefore seldom wasted. Toasted flat bread broken into small pieces and soaked in stock remains the basis of several homely Levantine dishes. They commonly go under the name *fatah* in Arabic and echo *tharid,* the favourite dish of Muhammad, which was sometimes made with soaked bread instead of wheat.

and lay out on a serving dish.
3. Pour 1 litre of the hot cooking liquid over the pieces of bread and leave to absorb. Lay half of the cooked chickpeas on the soaked bread.
4. Take half of the remaining cooked chickpeas and crush them into a paste. Place in a saucepan with the lemon juice and sesame seed paste. Blend together until the mixture resembles a thick sauce, adding water if necessary. Pour the sauce into the serving dish over the bread.
5. Fry the pine nuts until browned. Scatter the nuts and drizzle the pine nut-infused butter over the dish.
6. Garnish with the remaining whole chickpeas and chopped parsley.

FATAH WITH CHICKEN

1 small chicken
200g (1 cup) rice
2 flat bread loaves
Juice of 1 lemon
45g (3 tablespoons) sesame seed paste
15g (1 tablespoon) butter
65g (½ cup) pine nuts
2 garlic cloves, crushed
Salt and pepper, to season

1. Boil the chicken for 10 minutes. Remove the bird and throw away the liquid. Place the chicken in a pan of

fresh boiling water, season with salt and pepper, cover and cook on a medium heat for 30 minutes. Set the cooking liquid aside and remove the bones from the chicken and shred.

2. Combine the sesame seed paste, lemon juice and a little water to make a white sauce.

3. Rinse the rice in a sieve. Place in a saucepan, cover with water and bring to the boil. Reduce heat, cover and cook for 30 minutes.

4. Chop the bread into bite-sized pieces and lay out on a serving dish. Pour the white sauce and 500ml (2 cups) of the hot cooking liquid over the pieces of bread and leave to absorb.

5. Lay the cooked rice on top of the soaked bread followed by a layer of shredded chicken.

6. Fry the pine nuts and garlic with clarified butter until browned. Scatter the pine nuts and drizzle the garlic and nut-infused butter over the dish before serving.

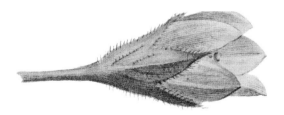

FATAH WITH AUBERGINES

8 baby aubergines
200g (7 ounces) lamb, chopped
2 flat bread loaves
250ml (1 cup) yogurt
4 garlic cloves, crushed
30g (2 tablespoons) clarified butter
Oil, to fry
130g (1 cup) pine nuts
Salt and pepper, to season
Coriander, to garnish

1. Boil the meat for 10 minutes. Remove and throw away the liquid. Place the meat in a saucepan and cover with fresh boiling water. Season and cook for 45 minutes.

2. Peel the aubergines and fry them in hot oil for several minutes. Transfer them to the pot with the meat.

3. Chop the bread into bite-sized pieces and lay out on a serving dish.

4. Mix the yogurt with 750ml (3 cups) of the hot cooking liquid in a bowl. Pour the mixture over the pieces of bread. Leave the bread to soak up the liquid.

5. Lay the aubergine and meat mixture on top of the soaked bread.

6. Fry the pine nuts and garlic until browned. Scatter the nuts and drizzle the pine nut and garlic-infused butter on the dish. Sprinkle with coriander and serve hot.

OPEN-FACED BREADS

Loaves of bread were often sprinkled with sea salt or toasted spices such as cumin, coriander, fenugreek or nigella seeds. Sometimes breads were prepared in a fashion similar to Italian foccacia. *Safiha,* as these breads are known in the Middle East to-day, are topped with everything from thyme to minced meat.

ZAHID'S ONION AND POMEGRANATE BREAD PUDDING

2 loaves flat bread, cut into
bite-sized pieces
2 onions, chopped
15ml (1 tablespoon) pomegranate
concentrate
2 teaspoons dried mint
45ml (3 tablespoons) olive oil
500ml (2 cups) water

1. Fry the onion in the oil until transparent.
2. Add the water and pomegranate juice to the pan, season and bring to the boil.
3. Transfer the bread to the pan and cook on a low heat until it has absorbed all the liquid.
4. Serve hot, sprinkled with the dried mint.

BREAKFAST BREAD PUDDING

1 litre (4 cups)whole milk
5 flat bread loaves, toasted

90g (6 tablespoons) honey
250ml (1 cup) cream

1. Pour the milk and cream into a tray so that it is 1cm deep and leave in a dark cool place for 12 hours minimum
2. Cut loaves longways and dip insides in tray, ensuring that outsides remain dry. Transfer to a serving dish and cover each loaf with honey.

BREAKFAST SAFIHA

Khoubiz dough for 4 loaves (see p. 56)
450g (1 pound) white cheese
2 eggs
1 tablespoon dried mint or
Salt and pepper for seasoning

1. Finely chop the cheese into small cubes and mix it with the beaten eggs.
2. Roll the dough into an oblong shape. Place on a baking tray and cover it with a thin layer of the cheese and egg mixture. Season with mint or salt and pepper.
3.Place in a pre-heated oven at 250C (500F) for 10 minutes.

THYME

Wild thyme grew all over the ancient Near East. *Thymus vulgaris,* known as *Zatar* in Arabic, has been a ubiquitous herb in the cuisine of the Near East since ancient times. Its essential oil, thymol, was used by the ancient Egyptians in their embalming process. This easily grown and decorative bush was appreciated for its insect-repelling qualities as well as an ingredient in a myriad of dishes. Thyme remains an essential component of the *bouquet garni* and of 'mixed herbs'. As Suyuti said that thyme was good to relieve indigestion. In fact, the Bedouin nomads of Arabia used thyme to cure all sorts of digestive problems, including ulcers.

SAFIHA ANTIOCH

Khoubiz dough for 8 loaves (see p. 56)
1 cup Antioch spice mix (see p. 35)
250ml (1 cup) olive oil

1. Roll the dough into flat thin discs on a floured board and transfer to a baking tray.
2. Spread the oil evenly over each disc of dough then sprinkle with spices.
3. Bake in a pre-heated oven at 250C (500F) for 10 minutes.

MEAT AND PINE NUT SAFIHA

Khoubiz dough for 4 loaves (see p. 56)
450g (1 pound) veal or lamb, minced
30ml (2 tablespoons) pomegranate concentrate
30g (2 tablespoons) sesame seed paste
30ml (2 tablespoons) yogurt
4 onions, finely chopped
65g (½ cup) pine nuts
Salt and pepper

1. Season the minced meat with salt and pepper to taste and mix with the onion, pomegranate concentrate, yogurt and sesame seed paste.
2. Roll the dough into thin discs the size of a side plate and lay on a baking tray. Spread the meat mixture on to the dough discs and garnish with the pine nuts.
3. Bake in a pre-heated oven at 250C (500F) for about 10 minutes.

DAIRY

*'In cattle do you have a worthy lesson.
We give you to drink of that
which is in their bellies ... pure milk,
pleasant for those who drink it.'*

QURAN, THE BEE 16:66

DAIRY PRODUCE

'He made him ride on the high places of the earth, and he ate the produce of the field; and he made him suck honey out of the rock, and oil out of the flinty rock. Curds from the herd, and milk from the flock.' DEUTERONOMY 32:13–14

Dairy produce was an essential source of protein in the ancient world. Descriptions of a *'promised land'* allude to a paradise, *'a land flowing with milk and honey'* [EXODUS 3:8]. Communities were reluctant to slaughter livestock, as it was far more economical to keep animals and benefit from their labour and by-products. Although sheep and goats were the most popular livestock, the nomadic pastoralists of the Near East also kept cows and camels. The Hebrews did not drink milk after infancy, but they did make good use of its by-products. Muhammad described an unearthly *'river of milk, whose taste never changes'* [QURAN, VICTORY 47:15] in the Garden of Eden, a far cry from the cocktail of harmful bacteria that milk quickly becomes if left unpasteurised and at room temperature. However, some of these bacteria play an important role in the transformation of milk into the more easily stored cheese, butter and yogurt. This produce provided much of the protein in the diet of the Holy Landers, and was an important source of calcium. However, despite their nutritional value, dairy products have a high fat content and should therefore be consumed in moderation. In addition, temperance is advised for the millions of lactose-intolerant people around the world. Furthermore, Jewish dietary law regulates the consumption of dairy produce, specifying that it should not be eaten with meat.

BUTTER

'Abu Nufaim has related that the Prophet, may Allah bless him and grant him peace, once said to Ayesha, 'I love you more than I do butter and honey.' SAYING OF MUHAMMAD RELATED BY ABU NU'AIM, IN AS SUYUTI

The Hebrews, like the nomadic pastoralists before them, churned butter from the milk of their livestock. The process is mentioned in the Book of Proverbs, *'as pressing milk produces curds, pressing the nose produces blood'* [PROVERBS 30:33]. Trading records from the Hittite Empire, which flourished in modern Turkey from 1900 BC for seven hundred years, even state the price of butter at 'one shekel per zipittani', indicating that this rich and nutritious product was a valued luxury in the ancient world. Butter is made by churning milk, a process which disturbs the creamy emulsion, forcing the fat into a mass and releasing buttermilk. It is then cleaned and often salted. However, it remains subject to oxidation and therefore will ultimately go bad. A common method of further delaying this deterioration is to clarify the fat. The result is a rendered butter known as *ghee* or *samna*. Ali, Muhammad's principal disciple, is reported to have said, *'People will never find anything more excellent than ghee'* [SAYING OF MUHAMMAD RELATED BY ABU NU'AIM, IN AS SUYUTI].

CLARIFIED BUTTER

450g (1 pound) butter

1. Gently heat the butter in a pan, without stirring.
2. Skim off the white foam that forms on top of the liquified fat.
3. At this point the fat solids should have separated from the liquid. The mixture can be left to cool and the liquid poured off. Alternatively, the mixture can be further heated until the liquid evaporates, leaving only the fat solids behind. The clarified butter can be stored in an airtight container and used as required.

YOGURT

'It was related that Ibn Abbas said: "Umm Hufaid, the aunt of Ibn Abbas, sent some dried yogurt, ghee and a mastigar to the Prophet as a gift. The Prophet ate the dried yogurt and ghee but left the mastigar because he did not like it."' SAYING OF MUHAMMAD RELATED BY AL BUKHARI

Yogurt is reputed to have been one of Muhammad's favourite foods. This delicious fermented milk keeps longer than the beverage, and is more digestible to the lactose-intolerant as its sugar is broken down to lactic acid. This acid gives the substance a distinctively sour taste, which itself varies according to the type of milk used. Goat and sheep's milk yogurt are the most stable types and are therefore the most suitable for Levantine cooking, although cow's milk yogurt can be stabilised with the addition of a little cornflour. Yogurt remains a staple in the Near East, where it is consumed in many forms: as a beverage, *ayran,* or as *lebne,* a sort of yogurt cheese. Long associated with longevity, live yogurt is said to ease fungal and yeast infections as well as relieve the symptoms of hay fever. Furthermore, yogurt is is a low-fat alternative to other dairy products such as cream and cheese.

YOGURT

2 litres (8 cups) whole milk, untreated
250ml (1 cup) cream
30ml (2 tablespoons) yogurt starter

1. Place the milk in a non-aluminium heavy-based saucepan over a medium heat until warm.
2. Place the yogurt starter and cream in a bowl and add 4 tablespoons of milk. Blend and bind the 2 mixtures.
3. Cover with a heavy cloth and leave undisturbed in a dark place at room temperature for 6 hours to set.
4. Transfer to a cool place and leave to set for several hours before serving.

LEBNE

2 litres (8 cups) whole milk, untreated
250ml (1 cup) cream
30ml (2 tablespoons) yogurt starter
Salt

1. Place the milk in a non-aluminium heavy-based saucepan over a medium heat until warm.
2. Place the yogurt starter in a bowl and add 4 tablespoons of milk. Blend and slowly bind the 2 mixtures.
3. Cover with a heavy cloth and leave undisturbed in a dark place at room temperature for 6 hours to set.
4. Transfer to a cool place and leave undisturbed for several hours.
5. Pour the chilled yogurt into a colander lined with thin muslin or cheese cloth to allow the whey to drain off. Sprinkle with salt and leave in a cool place for 24 hours or more, depending on the desired consistency of the cheese.
6. Lay the lebne out on a tray and leave for several hours. At this stage the lebne is ready to be eaten. It can be spread on bread.
7. Alternatively, while in the tray, the lebne can be cut into squares and each square rolled into a walnut-sized ball. These lebne balls can be stored in glass jars filled with olive oil.

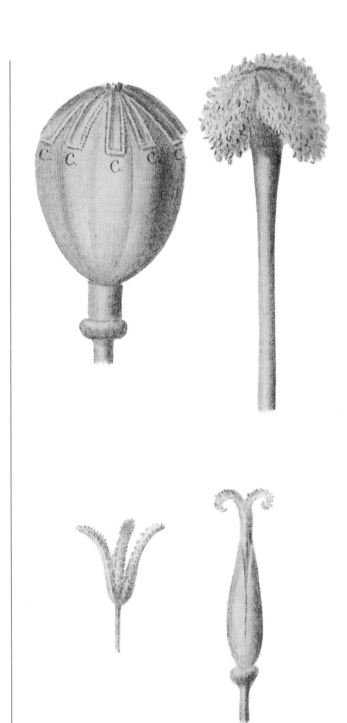

CHEESE

'I once offered the Prophet, may Allah bless him and grant him peace, some toasted cheese and he ate then went out to do the prayer without doing wudu.' SAYING OF MUHAMMAD RELATED BY AL TIRMIDH IN ASH SHAMA'IL, IN AS SUYUTI

The first evidence of cheese-making has been found in Sumeria, modern-day Iraq, about three thousand years before Christ. Depictions of cheese-making have also been found in Egyptian tombs. However, it is most likely that herdsmen accidentally discovered how to make cheese by storing milk on journeys in pouches made from animal skin. Movement, combined with the bacteria present in the animal skin, typically a stomach, would have resulted in a product quite similar to modern cottage cheese. In the Holy Land, cheese was produced from several animals, including cows, sheep and goats. Unlike today, most cheeses were made from goat and sheep milk. Cheese was a valuable source of protein and calcium, a way of preserving and concentrating the nutritional value of milk. As Suyuti even said that melted cheese was good for stomach ulcers. As a general rule, cheeses of the Eastern Mediterranean are soft and white and include what are known in the West as feta and haloumi.

ARAB CHEESE JIBIN

4 litres (16 cups) whole milk
1 rennet or junket tablet
30ml (2 tablespoons) warm water
Salt

1. Gently heat the milk in a heavy-based non-aluminium saucepan until warm.
2. Dissolve the rennet tablet in the warm water. Add to milk, stir well and remove the pan from heat.
3. Cover the saucepan with a lid and then a heavy cloth. Leave to stand undisturbed in a warm place for 4 hours.
4. Tip the cheese into a sieve and separate the curds from the whey. Press down on the curds and discard the liquid whey.
5. Lightly salt to eat immediately or heavily salt to store in brine-filled airtight jars. Soak to remove excess salt before serving.

MIZITHRA CHEESE

2 litres (8 cups) whole milk
2 rennet or junket tablets
15ml (1 tablespoon) water
Salt

1. Heat the milk in a heavy-based non-aluminium saucepan. Stir continuously. Once lukewarm, add the salt.
2. Crush the rennet tablets and dissolve in the water. Slowly add to the milk, stirring continuously but very gently. Remove from the heat and leave to stand undisturbed for thirty minutes.
3. Break up the curds with a whisk and leave to resettle.
4. Line a colander or a sieve with muslin or a thin piece of cloth and stand it over a large bowl. Spoon the curds into the colander. Leave to drain for 30 minutes. The bowl below should collect most of the whey.
5. Tie the corners of the cloth and leave the curds to hang undisturbed at room temperature for 6 hours.
6. Transfer the curds back to the colander and bowl and leave in a cool place for 12 hours.
7. Remove from the cloth and store the cheese in a sealed glass container in a cool place.

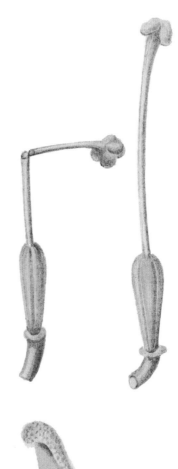

Mount Tabor from the Plain of Esdraelon

SIMPLE &
SIDE DISHES

'Moses,' you the Israelites said,
'we will no longer put up with
this monotonous diet.
Call on your Lord to give us some
of the varied produce of the earth,
green herbs and cucumbers, corn
and lentils and onions.'

QURAN, THE COW 2:61

SIMPLE & SIDE DISHES

The midday meal was a simple affair for people in the ancient Levant. Typically, it would have consisted of bread, olives, cheese and perhaps a simple cold dish. It was often eaten in the shade of a tree and followed by a short siesta as a break from the day's agricultural toil. The dishes in this chapter are designed to be suitable for lunch, as a traditional main course appetizer or to be eaten in the Lebanese way; that is, as *mezze*. *Mezze* usually comprises several dishes, up to a hundred in some cases, shared around the table. They bear a relation to Spanish *tapas*, which are undoubtedly a culinary legacy of the Arabs' eight-hundred-year-long Iberian sojourn, but differ in that *tapas* are generally eaten in bars. Levantine *mezze* are not eaten with alcohol. *Mezze* can be the sole component of a meal, may precede the main dishes or be eaten as side dishes with the principal hot dishes.

BITTER HERBS & SALADS

'In the second month on the fourteenth day, at twilight, they shall keep it, they shall eat it with unleavened bread and bitter herbs.' NUMBERS 9:11

The original green salad – the 'bitter herbs' of the Passover meal – probably consisted of lettuce, endive, parsley, cress, sorrel, lovage, rocket, mint and dandelion leaves. Wild versions of these plants would have all had a bitter taste due to their high oxalic acid content. Over the centuries they have been cultivated to be more palatable and therefore no longer seem as sour. The Jewish salad of bitter herbs was adapted according to the availability of these herbs and leaf vegetables. It is stated in Genesis that God has given his people *'every green herb for food'* [GENESIS 1:30]. A variation of bitter herbs was eaten in Egypt, where it was mixed with mustard and eaten with bread. *Maror*, as they are known in Hebrew, are still eaten to this day at the Jewish feast of the Passover to commemorate the bitter experiences of the Hebrews as slaves in Egypt. Although this salad has been widely interpreted through the ages, it is traditionally made up of leaf vegetables such as lettuce, endive and chicory, and aromatic herbs such as parsley and mint, along with various wild plants. The leaves are sometimes dressed simply in salted water to symbolise the tears of the enslaved Hebrews.

SALAD OF MIXED BITTER GREENS

10 fresh mint leaves
4 cups mixed greens such as rocket, endive, watercress, parsley dandelion greens, lovage and sorrel
60ml (4 tablespoons) olive oil
30ml (2 tablespoons) vinegar
1 garlic clove, crushed
½ teaspoon mustard seeds
Salt

1. Lightly toast the mustard seeds, leave to cool and grind in a pestle and mortar.
2. Whisk the vinegar, salt, garlic and mustard seeds together and slowly add in the oil.
3. Wash and dry the leaves. Tear into bite-sized pieces. Place in a serving bowl, dress the leaves with the sauce, toss and serve immediately.

BASIL

'Whoever is offered sweet basil should not refuse it, for it is easy to take and has a pleasing scent.' SAYING OF MUHAMMAD RELATED BY AL BUKHARI

Valued for its sweet scent and carminative qualities, basil has been a highly esteemed herb since antiquity. *Ocimum basilicum* is thought to be native to North East Africa, as well as Asia. It has been cultivated in the Eastern Mediterranean since ancient times and was also well-known to the Greeks and the Romans. Today it is primarily associated with Southern European cooking, but is also very important in Middle Eastern cuisine and is reported to have been a favourite of Muhammad. The delicate aroma of basil is lost when the herb is dried.

LAMB'S LETTUCE SALAD

100g (3 ½ ounces) lamb's lettuce (*mâche*)
1 stick celery, finely chopped
1 romaine lettuce
1 spring onion, chopped
8 basil leaves, torn
60ml (4 tablespoons) olive oil
30ml (2 tablespoons) apple vinegar
Salt and pepper

1. Wash and dry the lamb's lettuce and romaine leaves. Tear the romaine leaves into bite-size pieces and break up any clumps of lamb's lettuce.
2. Place the leaves in a serving bowl with the chopped celery, spring onion and torn basil leaves. Dress with vinegar and season. Toss a little and pour the oil onto the salad. Toss again until all the vegetables are coated in oil. Serve immediately.

SALAD OF DANDELION LEAVES

450g (1 pound) dandelion leaves
8 basil leaves, torn
1 clove garlic, crushed
Juice of 1 lemon
60ml (4 tablespoons) olive oil
Salt and pepper

1. Wash and chop the dandelion leaves into small pieces. Place in a saucepan of salted water and bring to the boil. Reduce the heat to a medium setting and cook for 15 minutes. Drain and rinse in cold water, drain and squeeze out any excess liquid.
2. Mash the garlic and salt together with a fork, add the lemon juice, season and beat in the oil.

3. Transfer the leaves to a serving bowl along with the torn basil leaves and toss in the dressing. Serve with flat bread.

WHITE PARSLEY SALAD

1 cup parsley, finely chopped
1 onion, finely chopped
30ml (2 tablespoons) sesame seed paste
30ml (2 tablespoons) lemon juice
30ml (2 tablespoons) olive oil
Salt

1. Mix the onion and parsley together in a serving bowl and season.
2. Whisk the lemon, sesame seed paste and oil together into a white sauce.

Dress the parsley and onion with the white sauce. Serve as an appetizer or as a side dish with kibbeh or fish.

PARSLEY

The repeated mention of the generalised word 'herbs' in the Bible is thought to refer to those herbs which were abundant in the Holy Land. Parsley is perhaps the most widely-used herb in the contemporary Levant, as indeed it was in ancient times. *Petroselinum crispum* was a common feature all over the ancient world. Dedicated to Persephone in Greece, it was said to have accompanied her to the underworld. A versatile herb, it can be used in a multitude of Levantine dishes. Parsley is an anti-oxidant and is rich in iron, carotenoids and vitamin C. Additionally, it can function as a natural breath freshener and therefore often accompanies garlic and onions in Levantine cooking. As Suyuti wrote that it was sometimes used as a remedy for toothache. The parsley specified in these recipes is the flat-leaved variety, widely known as Italian parsley, which is native to the Near East.

ENDIVE

'Eat endives … for there is not a single day in which some of the drops of the water of the Garden of Eden do not fall on them.' SAYING OF MUHAMMAD RELATED BY ABU NU'AIM, IN AS SUYUTI

There is much confusion about endives and chicory, but it is generally agreed that chicory is a perennial herb with short hairs and endive is hairless. The curly-leafed *Chicorum endiva*, known as chicory in the United States and as endives in Europe, is normally eaten raw in salads. Endives were known to the Egyptians and were cultivated by the Romans. Their acerbic-like taste has led to the suggestion that they were included in the 'bitter herbs' of Passover. Endives originate in the Near East but palatable chicory, or *Chicorum intybus,* may well not have been cultivated until as late as the sixteenth century. Although endives are normally eaten in salads, they are also included cooked in Levantine cuisine.

ENDIVE SALAD

225g (½ pound) endive
½ large onion, finely chopped
4 tablespoons parsley, chopped
1 clove garlic, crushed
30ml (2 tablespoons) lemon juice
45ml (3 tablespoons) olive oil
Salt and pepper

1. Wash the endives and chop finely. Cook in boiling water for 15 minutes. Drain well.
2. Place in a serving bowl with the chopped onion, parsley and crushed garlic. Toss in oil and lemon juice, season with salt and pepper and leave to cool before serving.

CUCUMBER

'We remember the fish we used to eat in Egypt for nothing, the cucumbers, the melons, the leeks, the onions, and the garlic, but now all our strength is dried up, and there is nothing at all but this manna.' NUMBERS 11:5–6

A creeping cucurbit, *Cucumis sativus* was widely enjoyed by the Hebrews in Egypt. In the ancient Holy Land cucumbers were grown in fields and were commonly small and irregular in shape, somewhat similar to what are today known as ridge cucumbers. The Romans were the first to have the idea of growing them in hothouses, owing to the vegetable's extreme intolerance to frost. Millennia of grafting and protection have produced what is erroneously known in the West as the English cucumber. They are mentioned extensively throughout the Bible, the Quran and the Hadith where Muhammad is reported to have enjoyed eating them with dates, demonstrating their prominence as a feature in the ancient diet. Cucumbers are composed of ninety six per cent water, are low in fat, and also contain sterols, which are said to lower cholesterol. They are also believed to be beneficial to the intestines if eaten at the beginning of a meal. Cucumbers are a refreshing food in hot climates and are often teamed with yogurt in Mediterranean cuisine. Mostly eaten raw in salads, immature cucumbers can also be pickled in vinegar and are often seasoned with dill.

CUCUMBER SALAD

1 large or 4 small cucumbers
1 spring onion, chopped
10 black olives
1 ½ teaspoons sumac
1 teaspoon salt
125ml (½ cup) lemon juice

1. Peel and cube the cucumber. Pit and halve the olives.
2. Place the cucumber in a serving bowl and mix with the chopped spring onion.
3. Dress the vegetables with lemon juice, season with salt, sprinkle with sumac and garnish with olive halves.

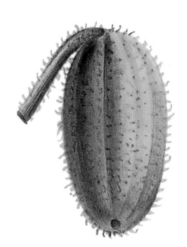
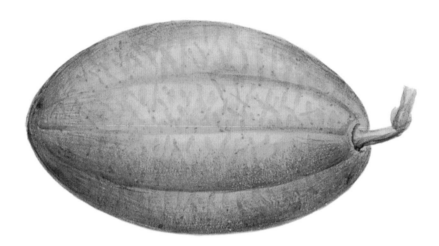

'And daughter Zion is left like a booth in a vineyard, like a shelter in a cucumber field, like a besieged city.' ISAIAH 1:8

CUCUMBER AND LETTUCE SALAD

1 romaine lettuce
4 spring onions, chopped
1 large or 4 small cucumbers
½ cup parsley, finely chopped
2 tablespoons dry mint
2 tablespoons chives, chopped
1 garlic clove, crushed
Juice of ½ a lemon
60ml (¼ cup) olive oil
Salt and pepper

1. Wash and dry the lettuce, tear into bite-sized pieces. Peel and dice the cucumber and place in a serving bowl with the lettuce, chopped onion, chives, parsley and mint.
2. Mash the crushed garlic and salt and pepper together in a small bowl. Mix in the lemon juice and then the oil. Dress the salad and serve immediately.

CUCUMBER AND FETA SALAD

1 large cucumber
12 black olives
30ml (2 tablespoons) lemon juice
100g (3 ½ ounces) feta or goat's cheese
½ teaspoon dried mixed herbs
45ml (3 tablespoons) olive oil
30ml (2 tablespoons) vinegar

1. Place the peeled, de-seeded and cubed cucumber in a serving bowl.
2. Gently mix with the vinegar, season with salt and pepper and dress with the oil and olives. Crumble the feta onto the salad. Serve chilled with flat bread.

CUCUMBER AND GOAT'S CHEESE SALAD

100g (3 ½ ounces) goat's cheese
1 cucumber, peeled and diced
2 romaine lettuce hearts
1 spring onion, sliced
2 tablespoons mint, chopped
45ml (3 tablespoons) olive oil
30ml (2 tablespoons) vinegar
1 flat bread
1 teaspoon sumac, salt and pepper

1. Place the cubed cheese in a serving bowl with the peeled and diced cucumber, lettuce hearts, sliced onion and chopped mint.
2. Break the bread into bite size pieces and lightly toast. Sprinkle the toast with sumac and set aside.
3. Season the salad with salt and pepper and dress with the vinegar and then the oil. Garnish with the toasted bread and serve immediately.

MELON

'The Prophet, may Allah bless him and grant him peace, used to eat melon together with fresh dates. He used to say "One drives out heat, the other, cold."' SAYING OF MUHAMMAD, RELATED BY AL TIRMIDHI IN AS SUYUTI

Melons have been cultivated in Egypt for about five thousand years. They were one of the foods lamented by the Hebrews after their exodus from Egypt. *Cucumis melo* is the botanical name for cucurbit melons, which are closely related to cucumbers and gourds. Watermelon, or *Citrullus lanatus*, depicted on the pyramids, is native to Africa. It served the Egyptians in many ways: as food, drink and medicine against fever. To this day, people use watermelons to help combat fever when medicine is unobtainable. Melon is also antibacterial and anticoagulant, and some varieties have been found to contain anti-carcinogenic agents. Melon is usually eaten as a refreshing appetiser, snack, or dessert, whilst watermelon seeds can also be roasted and salted.

THREE MELON SALAD

2 cups watermelon, cubed
2 cups cantaloupe, in balls
2 cups honey melon, in balls
1 tablespoon honey
Several sprigs of mint

1. Arrange half of the watermelon on a serving platter with balls of cantaloupe and honey melon.
2. Blend the honey with the rest of the watermelon to make a sauce and pour over the serving platter. Garnish with mint and serve immediately.

MELON, FETA AND DATE SALAD

125g (4 ounces) feta cheese
1 large melon
4 ripe dates, chopped

1. Peel and core the melon and cut the flesh into bite-sized chunks. Place the melon on a serving platter with the chopped dates.
2. Scatter crumbled feta over the fruit. Serve immediately. Garnish with mint if desired.

BEETROOT

'Umm al-Mundhir said: God's messenger came in to visit me accompanied by 'Ali when we had some ripening dates hung up. He began to eat, and 'Ali along with him, but God's messenger said to 'Ali, "Stop, 'Ali, for you are convalescing." I then prepared some beetroot and barley for them and the Prophet said, "Take some of this, 'Ali, for it will be more beneficial for you."' SAYING OF MUHAMMAD RELATED BY AHMAD, AL TIRMIDHI AND IBN MAJAH, IN AS SUYUTI

Beetroot evolved from wild sea beet, which was a common seashore plant in the Eastern Mediterranean. Although *Beta vulgaris* is not specifically mentioned in the Bible, its root was such a common table vegetable in Ancient Rome that red beets are still known as Roman Beets. Muhammad and his followers appreciated the benefits of this root vegetable, which is a good source of potassium. Red Beetroot's magnificent purple hue has caused it to be used as a dye throughout history.

YOGURT AND PARSLEY BEETROOT

450g (1 pound) young beetroot
30ml (2 tablespoons) lemon juice
30ml (2 tablespoons) olive oil
250ml (1 cup) plain yogurt
2 tablespoons parsley, chopped
Salt and pepper

1. If using fresh beetroot, cut off their tops and cook in a pan of boiling water for 40 minutes. Leave to cool, peel and slice into rounds.
2. Whisk the lemon juice and 1 table-spoon of the yogurt together, season with salt and pepper and slowly blend in the oil until absorbed. Add the rest of the yogurt.
3. Place the beets in a serving dish, cover with the sauce and serve garnished with parsley.

BEETROOT WITH YOGURT AND MINT

450g (1 pound) young beetroot
125ml (½ cup) plain yogurt
1 tablespoon dried mint

1. If using fresh beetroot, cut off their tops and cook in a pan of boiling water for 40 minutes. Leave to cool, peel and slice into rounds.

2. Arrange the slices in layers on a serving dish and cover with yogurt.

3. Leave in a cool place for 1 hour and sprinkle with mint just before serving.

BEETROOT AND SESAME SALAD

450g (1 pound) young beetroot
60ml (4 tablespoons) sesame seed paste
60ml (4 tablespoons) plain yogurt
60ml (4 tablespoons) olive oil
30ml (2 tablespoons) lemon juice
2 tablespoons parsley, chopped
4 tablespoons walnuts, chopped
Salt and pepper

1. If using fresh beetroot, cut off their tops and cook in a pan of boiling water for 40 minutes. Leave to cool, peel and slice into rounds.

2. Whisk the yogurt, sesame seed paste, lemon juice and salt together and then slowly add the olive oil. Place the beets in a mixing bowl, dress with the sauce and garnish with the chopped nuts and parsley.

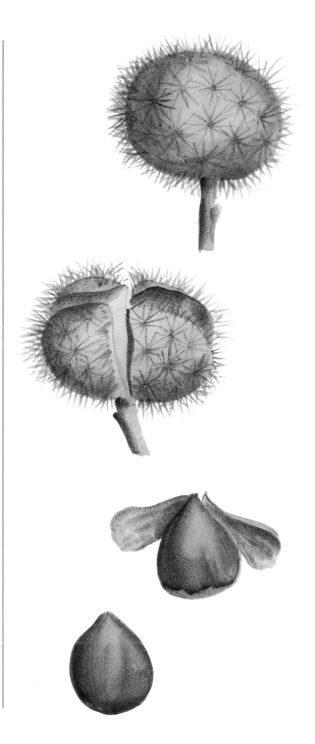

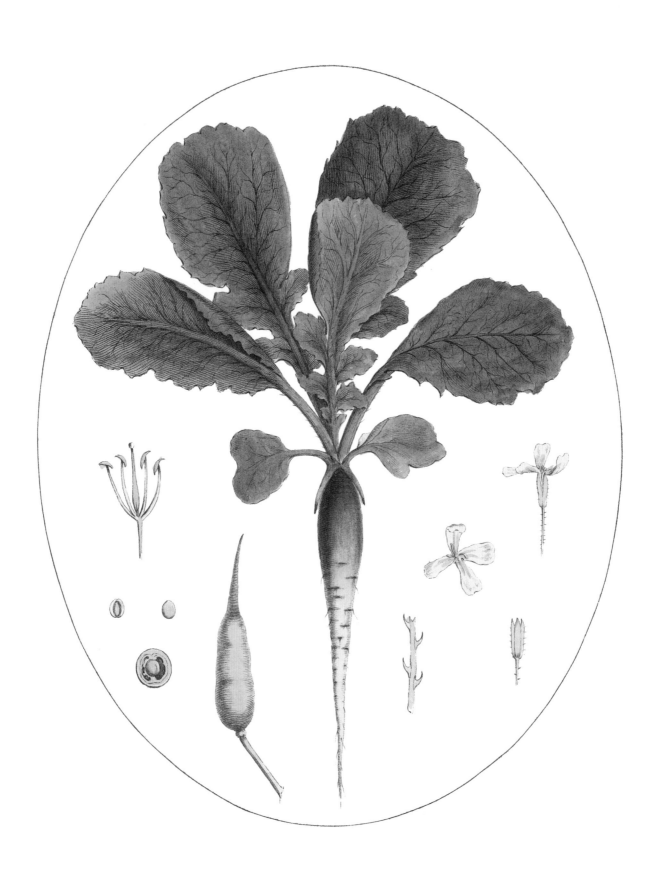

RADISH

'Whoever enjoys eating radishes but is unaware of their smell should remember the Prophet, may Allah bless him and grant him peace, whenever he first nibbles at or eats one.' MUHAMMAD, RELATED BY SA`ID IBN AL-MASSIYIB IN AS SUYUTI

While radishes are not mentioned directly in the Bible, they are thought to have emerged in the Eastern Mediterranean region around 2000 BC and were a common table vegetable in ancient Egypt and thus probably also in Palestine. Herodotus remarked that radishes were part of the staple diet of the masses building the pyramids. Although *Raphanus sativus* is no longer known in its wild state, as it was in the classical world, the fleshy root is usually consumed and contains a reasonable amount of vitamin C.

RADISH AND CUCUMBER SALAD

1 large cucumber
1 spring onion, sliced
4 radishes
15ml (1 tablespoon) olive oil
30ml (2 tablespoons) lemon juice
1 garlic clove, crushed
Salt and pepper

1. Peel and cube the cucumber. Chop the washed and prepared radishes into rounds. Place the cucumber and radish in a serving bowl with the slices of spring onion.
2. Toss the vegetables in the lemon juice, season with salt and pepper and add the olive oil. Toss again and serve.

RADISH AND ORANGE SALAD

12 radishes
2 oranges
Juice of ½ a lemon
¼ teaspoon orange flower water
1 tablespoon honey
Pepper

1. Grate the washed and prepared radishes into shreds and place in a serving bowl.
2. Peel the oranges and slice them into rounds. Slice each round into 6 or 8 chunks and transfer to the serving bowl with the radishes.
3. Dress with lemon juice, orange flower water and honey, and season with pepper.

VINE

'Once there were two men, to one of whom we gave two vineyards set about with palm trees and watered by a running stream, with a cornfield lying in between. Each of the vineyards yielded an abundant crop.' QURAN, THE CAVE 18:32

The vine is the first cultivated plant recorded in the Bible. Egyptian drawings indicate that it was also cultivated by the banks of the Nile. Its prominence in Biblical times is undisputed, where grapes were regarded as a symbol of God's generous bounty. *Vitis vinifera* is one of the oldest cultivated fruit crops in the world. Evidence of this has been found at Jericho, dated at about 3200 BC. The leaves of the vine are edible and can be blanched and stuffed with various fillings. Such dishes were perfected at the Ottoman court and are still prominent in Turkish and Levantine cuisine. The fruit of the vine is very versatile and was put to many uses in the ancient Levant. Commonly grapes were eaten fresh, but were also dried to make raisins, pressed for juice or fermented to make wine and vinegar. Today in the Holy Land, grape juice is still boiled down to make syrup called *dibs*, not unlike the Roman condiment *liquamen*.

IBRAHIM'S FINGERS

300g (10 ½ ounces) vine leaves
450g (1 pound) quail meat
or 3-4 quails
100g (3 ½ ounces) rice
Juice of 2 lemons
Salt

1. Boil the quails for 10 minutes, remove the meat and throw away the water. Roast the quail in an oven for 20 minutes. Leave to cool.

2. Remove the meat from the quails and chop finely. Keep the bones aside. Mix the meat with the rice and salt.
2. Place fresh vine leaves in a saucepan of boiling water for 2 minutes, remove with a slotted spoon and plunge in cold water. If using vine leaves preserved in brine, plunge them in boiling water for 1 minute to make them malleable.
3. Lay out each leaf on a board and place a strip of the mixture in the centre of each, mould with fingers

if necessary. Fold the 2 ends over the mixture and roll the sides around as if rolling a cigar. The ends should be sealed in the parcel and the vine leaf should resemble a forefinger.

4. Place the quail bones at the bottom of a saucepan. Carefully lay the vine leaves over the bones. Cover with water and lemon juice.

5. Push a lid down over the vines and secure with a weight. Cook on a low heat for 3 hours and serve hot.

STUFFED VINE LEAVES

1 medium onion, finely chopped
45ml (3 tablespoons) olive oil
45g (3 tablespoons) rice
1 tablespoon pine nuts
1 tablespoon raisins
1 tablespoon pomegranate concentrate
½ teaspoon cinnamon
½ lemon, thinly sliced
Juice of 1 lemon
Salt and pepper

1. Gently fry the pine nuts with olive oil until golden. Remove and set aside. Gently fry the onion with the same oil until soft. Add the rice, currants, pomegranate concentrate, cinnamon and season with salt and pepper. Heat through, return the pine nuts to the pan and set the mixture aside.

2. Place fresh vine leaves in a saucepan of boiling water for 2 minutes, remove with a slotted spoon and plunge in cold water. If using vine leaves preserved in brine, plunge them in boiling water for 1 minute to make them malleable.

3. Lay out each leaf on a board and place a strip of the mixture in the centre of each, mould with fingers if necessary. Fold the 2 ends over the mixture and roll the sides around as if rolling a cigar. The ends should be sealed in the parcel. The rolled leaf should resemble a forefinger or a cigar.

4. Pack the vine leaves into the bottom of a heavy-based pan. Cover with boiling water, a little oil and lemon juice. Secure a plate with a weight over the rolls to hold them in place.

5. Leave to simmer for 1 hour. Remove from pan, drain and leave to cool. Serve with yogurt.

'In my dream, there was a vine before me; and on the vine were three branches: as soon as it budded its blossoms shot forth, and the clusters ripened into grapes.'
GENESIS 40:9–11

SESAME

This perennial herb was cultivated in the ancient world for its oil-producing seeds. Thirty boxes of sesame seeds were found in the tomb of Tutankhamun. Although no such aged specimens have been recovered at archaeological sites in Mesopotamia, the seeds are mentioned by Herodotus, who remarked that they were used in cooking in Babylonia, and in descriptions of Nebuchadnezzar's palace. Indeed, many of the recipes in the thirteenth-century cookery book *Kitab al Tabikh* specify this easily stored oil for frying. The seeds themselves can be eaten, their oil extracted or made into a paste known today as *tahina*. Since the oil is a very rich source of polyunsaturated fatty acids and vitamin E, it is often considered to be an important food in the fight against the ageing process. Additionally, sesame seeds are rich in vitamin C and contain riboflavin.

NORTHERN MOUTABAL

4 large aubergines
125ml (½ cup) yogurt
60ml (4 tablespoons) sesame seed paste
60ml (4 tablespoons) olive oil
Salt

1. Wash the aubergine and pierce the skin all over with a fork. Place in the oven at 250C (500F) and cook until the skin is black and blistering, about 45 minutes. Alternatively the aubergines can be barbecued.
2. Leave to stand until cool enough to handle and make an incision length-ways down the aubergine. Scoop out the flesh and place in a mixing bowl.
Mash the aubergine flesh and add the sesame seed paste and yogurt. Season with salt and mix well.
3. Transfer to a serving dish and drizzle with olive oil. Serve with flat bread.

CAVIAR OF AUBERGINES

450g (1 pound) aubergine
45ml (3 tablespoons) olive oil
Juice of ½ lemon
1 garlic clove, crushed
Salt

1. Wash the aubergine and pierce the skin all over with a fork. Place in the oven at 250C (500F) and cook until the skin is black and blistering, about 45 minutes. Alternatively the aubergines can be cooked on a barbecue.
2. Leave to stand until cool enough to handle and make an incision length-ways down the aubergine. Scoop out the flesh and place in a mixing bowl. Mash the aubergine flesh in a bowl and add the oil, lemon juice and crushed garlic. Season and mix well.
3. Transfer to a serving dish and serve with flat bread.

POMEGRANATE BATERSCH

450g (1 pound) aubergine
45ml (3 tablespoons) extra virgin olive oil
125ml (½ cup) pomegranate concentrate
1 clove of garlic, crushed (optional)
½ cup parsley
Salt

1. Wash the aubergine and pierce the skin all over with a fork. Place in the oven at 250C (500F) and cook until the skin is black and blistering, about 45 minutes. Alternatively the aubergines can be cooked on a barbecue.
2. Leave to stand until cool enough to handle and make an incision length-ways down the aubergine. Scoop out the flesh and place in a mixing bowl. Mash the aubergine and add the pomegranate concentrate and garlic. Season with salt and mix well.
3. Transfer to a serving dish, drizzle with olive oil and garnish with parsley. Serve with flat bread.

ARTICHOKE

The globe artichoke, *Cyanara scolymus,* evolved from wild cardoons in the Mediterranean region, possibly Sicily. Artichokes were popular in ancient Rome where they were preserved with honey and vinegar and seasoned with cumin. It is likely that the Romans imported this thistle into their Levantine territories, where it grew easily. The origins of the word artichoke are obscure; it is possibly derived from the Arabic, meaning 'the thorn of the earth'. The vegetable known as *al qarshuf* in Arabic and *al cachofa* in Spanish was undoubtedly a relative of the artichoke and the cardoon. Artichokes can be delicious, but do require a certain amount of patience and preparation. They can be boiled, steamed, baked, fried, stuffed and used in soups. The petioles can be consumed but it is the hearts that are most prized; small young artichokes can be eaten in their entirety.

ARTICHOKES WITH OLIVE OIL

9 artichoke hearts
75ml (5 tablespoons) olive oil
Juice of 1 lemon
2 garlic cloves, chopped
Salt and pepper

1. To extract the hearts: remove the petioles, cut off the hard stalks and remove the fuzzy choke.
2. Place the hearts in a pan with the oil, lemon juice and garlic. Barely cover with water and simmer, uncovered, for 30 minutes.
3. Remove the hearts from the pan and transfer to a serving dish. Reduce the sauce, season and pour over the hearts. Leave to cool before serving.

ARTICHOKE SALAD

4 large artichokes
60ml (4 tablespoons) olive oil
Juice of ½ lemon
30ml (2 tablespoons) white vinegar
2 tablespoons parsley, chopped
Salt

1. To extract the hearts: remove the petioles, cut off the hard stems and remove the fuzzy choke.
2. Place the hearts in a saucepan of boiling water and leave to cook for 1 hour.
3. Slice the hearts and dress with the lemon juice, vinegar, oil, parsley and season. Leave to cool before serving.

MUSHROOMS AND TRUFFLES

'It was related that Safid Ibn Zaid said that the Messenger of God said : "The truffle is a kind of manna and its water heals the eyes."' SAYING OF MUHAMMAD, RELATED BY AL BUKHARI

Letters found during excavations at Mari show that the Mesopotamians appreciated fungi as early as 1800 BC. In classical writings, Euripides and Hippocrates both refer to cases of mushroom poisoning, and it was probably with the Roman mushrooms *boleti* that Agrippa poisoned her husband, the Emperor Claudius. As Suyuti wrote of the confusion between the poisonous and edible varieties of mushrooms; consequently, mushrooms of the *Agaricales* and *Boletales* varieties became common ingredients in Near Eastern cooking. Their strong taste and texture means they are often used in vegetarian cooking, but they have little real nutritional value save some vitamin B and some protein in certain species. Furthermore, they are known to have anticoagulant and antiviral properties. Desert truffles of the genus *Termania* and *Terfazia* were common in the East. They are known as *kama* or *faqa* in Arabic and the best are said to come from Damascus and the Gulf. They differ from European truffles in that they are found nearer to the surface, have a milder flavour and are generally less expensive. Desert truffles can be dried and reconstituted ; they may be found in some Middle Eastern stores.

MUSHROOM SALAD

450g (1 pound) small mushrooms
45ml (3 tablespoons) olive oil
1 tablespoon water
Juice of 1 lemon
1 teaspoon dried thyme
2 garlic cloves, crushed
4 tablespoons parsley, chopped
Salt and pepper

1. Wash and prepare the mushrooms. Heat the oil in a pan with a little water. Stir in the garlic, thyme and season with salt and pepper.
2. Add the mushrooms to the pan and cook for 15 minutes. Stir in the chopped parsley and lemon juice and transfer to a serving dish. Adjust seasonings and serve cold.

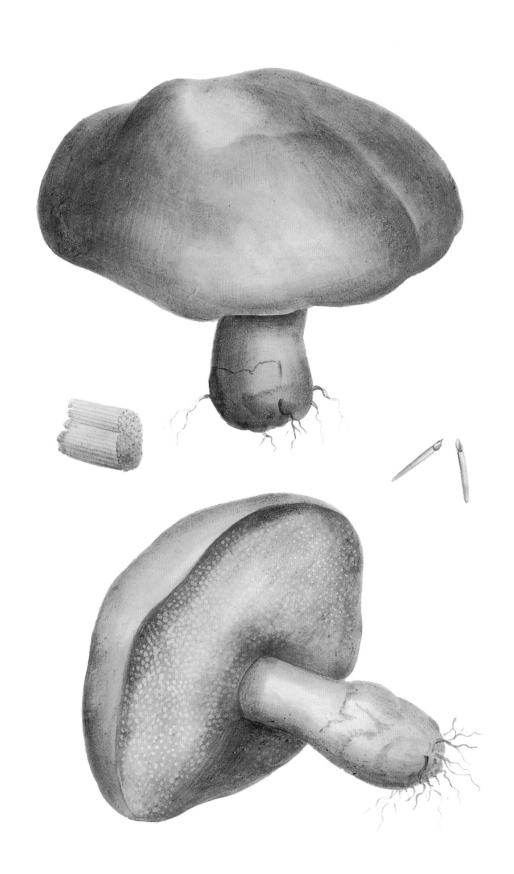

MUSHROOMS WITH CUMIN

225g (½ pound) mushrooms
30ml (2 tablespoons) extra virgin
olive oil
2 garlic cloves, crushed
1 teaspoon cumin
15ml (1 tablespoon) lemon juice
2 tablespoons coriander,
finely chopped
1 teaspoon thyme
1 teaspoon tarragon
Salt and pepper

1. Wash the mushrooms and
chop finely
2. Heat the oil in a pan and fry the
mushrooms with the crushed garlic
for about 5 minutes. Stir the cumin,
tarragon, thyme and lemon juice into
the pan and season with salt and pepper.
3. Reduce the pan to a very low heat
and cook for another 5 minutes,
stirring occasionally.
4. Transfer to a serving dish and stir
in the coriander. Leave to cool and
adjust seasonings.

DESERT TRUFFLE SALAD

450g (1 pound) desert truffles
90ml (6 tablespoons) olive oil
2 tablespoons parsley, chopped
1 clove garlic, crushed
Salt and pepper

1. Wash the truffles and place them
in a saucepan. Cover with water and
season with salt and pepper. Bring
to the boil and cook on a medium heat
for 1 hour.
2. Remove the truffles from the
saucepan, drain and cube. Be careful
to remove any grit that may be in the
interior air pockets. Place in a serving
bowl, drizzle with olive oil, mix with
the crushed garlic and chopped
parsley. Season, eat hot or cold.

TRUFFLES ANTIOC

100g truffles
450g (1 pound) lamb, minced
1 onion, chopped
Salt and pepper

1. Wash the truffles and place them in
a pan, cover with water and season
with salt and pepper. Bring to the boil
and cook on a medium heat for 1 hour.
2. Remove the truffles from the pan,
drain and cut into cubes.
3. Dry fry the minced lamb and onion
in a saucepan, season and cook until
browned. Add the truffles to the meat
and cook for about 10 minutes.
Serve hot.

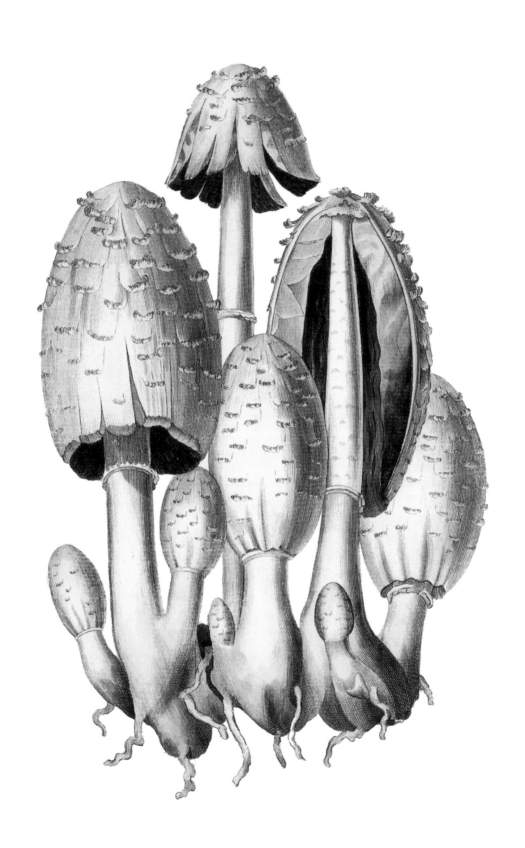

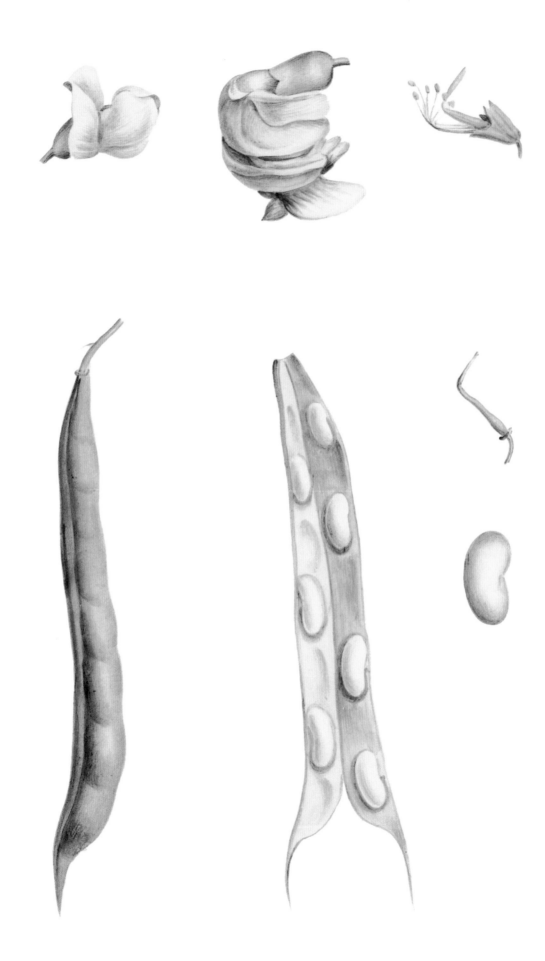

BEANS

'... and Barzilai the Gileadite of Rogelim, brought beds, basins, and earthen vessels, wheat, barley, meal, parched grain, beans and lentils.' II SAMUEL 17: 27–28

Although beans were generally distrusted and avoided by the upper echelons of society in the classical world, they constituted a major part of the Levantine diet, particularly as a protein source. They were easily stored by drying. The principal beans grown and eaten in the region were fava or broad beans, whereas the haricot or green bean actually originates in the Americas. It is unclear where exactly in South West Asia *Vicia faba,* or broad bean, first emerged, but the earliest archaeological evidence of fava beans has been found in the Holy Land and dates back to the Neolithic period, around 6500 BC. Fava beans were eaten dried and fresh in dishes such as *foul medames*, given to animals and even mixed ground into flour and combined with grains to make bread. They are composed of nearly twenty-five per cent protein when dried. Fresh beans contain more water but do have some vitamin C. They are a good source of fibre but are sometimes found to be indigestible. It is important to note that many people in the world are intolerant to fava bean. Favism causes a breakdown in red blood cells leading to anaemia and jaundice, which can prove fatal in some cases.

FAVA BEAN SALAD

450g (1 pound) fava beans
125 ml (½ cup) olive oil
125ml (½ cup) lemon juice
125ml (½ cup) sesame seed paste
½ teaspoon cumin
2 tablespoons parsley, chopped
Salt

1. If using dry beans, soak overnight.

Drain the beans, place in a saucepan and cover with boiling water. Cook dried beans for 1 hour 30 minutes, fresh beans for 30 minutes.
2. Whisk the sesame seed paste, lemon and oil together to make a white sauce.
3. Drain the beans and transfer them to a serving dish. Pour the sauce over the beans, season and mix well. Garnish with parsley and cumin. Serve cold.

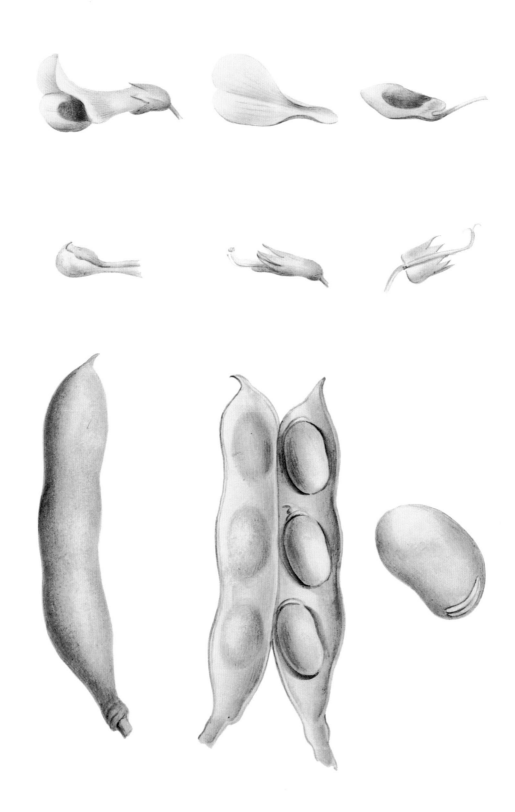

FAVA AND LEMON SALAD

450g (1 pound) fava beans
1 garlic clove, crushed
60ml (4 tablespoons) lemon juice
60ml (4 tablespoons) olive oil
4 tablespoons parsley, chopped
2 tablespoons scallions, chopped
½ lemon, cut into wedges
Salt

1. Drain the beans and place in a saucepan, cover, reduce heat and simmer for 1 hour. Add more water if necessary.
2. Place the garlic, lemon, oil, parsley and scallions in a bowl. Add in the cooked fava beans, season with salt and combine all the ingredients.
3. Garnish with lemon wedges and serve hot or cold with flat bread.

CORIANDER

'Now the manna was like coriander seed, and its appearance like that of bdellium.'
NUMBERS 11:7

This nutritious, aromatic herb originated in the Eastern Mediterranean, where archaeological evidence suggests it first appeared during the Neolithic age. The aromatic umbellifer *Coriandrum sativum* is also known as cilantro and Chinese parsley. It was valued by Egyptians, Greeks and Arabs alike for its small, spicy, white seeds, which can be used as both seasoning and medicine. Frequently mentioned in the Old Testament, coriander was also a favourite of the Hebrews. It was sometimes included in the 'bitter herbs' eaten at the Feast of Passover. The herb was so familiar to the ancient Hebrews in Old Testament times that when presented with previously unknown 'manna' in the wilderness, they initially described it as being *'like coriander seed, white'* [EXODUS 16:31]. Undoubtedly one of the most versatile herbs, every part of coriander is useful. The leaves are often used to flavour soups, salads and curries while the seeds are a common ingredient in Middle Eastern confectionery and sweets.

FAVA BEAN AND CORIANDER SALAD

450g (1 pound) fresh fava beans
4 spring onions, chopped
4 sprigs of coriander, chopped
250ml (1 cup) olive oil

1. Place the beans, coriander, onions and half of the oil in a saucepan and cover with 250ml (1 cup) of water.
2. Season, stir and cook on a medium heat for 30 minutes. Leave to cool and add the rest of the olive oil before serving if desired.

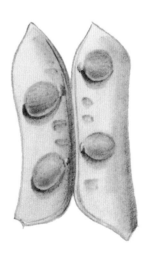

CHICKPEAS

Cicer arietinum, known as garbanzo beans in the United States, evolved from the wild somewhere in the Fertile Crescent about 6000 years ago. Chickpeas were an important pulse in the Levant. They are depicted on Phoenician glass jars and are mentioned in Hittite trading documents. A nutritious legume, they are composed of fifteen to twenty per cent protein. Chickpeas remain an important food in the Near East to this day. They are dried, cooked and prepared in various ways : served cold in salads, puréed and mixed with sesame seed paste (*tahina*). They are also served hot in soups and stews or ground into flour and mixed with grain to make bread. In order to make them more digestible, chickpeas can be cooked with a pinch of bicarbonate of soda or pomegranate skins.

CHICKPEA SALAD

450g (1 pound) chickpeas, soaked overnight
60ml (4 tablespoons) olive oil
Juice of 2 lemons
2 teaspoons cumin
2 garlic cloves, crushed
½ cup parsley, chopped
Salt

1. Drain the chickpeas and boil in salted water for 1 hour 30 minutes or until tender. Drain the chickpeas again and season with salt to taste.
2. Transfer the chickpeas to a serving bowl. Dress with lemon juice, olive oil, garlic, parsley and cumin. Adjust seasonings, mix well and serve cold.

CHICKPEA AND SESAME SALAD

300g (10½ ounces) chickpeas, soaked overnight
125 ml (½ cup) olive oil
125ml (½ cup) lemon juice
125ml (½ cup) sesame seed paste
½ teaspoon cumin
2 tablespoons parsley, chopped
Salt

1. Drain the chickpeas and place in a saucepan of salted boiling water. Cook for 1 hour 30 minutes or until tender.
2. Whisk the sesame seed paste, lemon juice and oil together to make a white sauce.
3. Drain the chickpeas and transfer to a serving dish. Pour the sauce over the chickpeas, season and mix well. Garnish with parsley. Serve cold with olive oil.

HUMMUS WITH CUMIN

90g (½ cup) chickpeas,
soaked overnight with 15ml
(1 tablespoon) bicarbonate of soda
125ml (½ cup) olive oil
½ teaspoon cumin

1. Drain the chickpeas and place in
a saucepan of salted boiling water.
Cook for 1 hour 30 minutes or
until tender.
2. Drain the chickpeas and blend into a
puree with the oil and cumin. Season
with salt and serve garnished with
whole chickpeas or parsley accompanied by flat bread.

HUMMUS WITH SESAME

225g (½ pound) chickpeas, soaked
overnight
45ml (3 tablespoons) sesame seed paste
45ml (3 tablespoons) lemon juice
Salt

1. Drain the chickpeas and place in a
saucepan of salted boiling water.
Cook for 1 hour 30 minutes or
until tender.
2. Drain the chickpeas and blend to a
puree with the sesame seed paste and
lemon juice. Season and serve
garnished with whole chickpeas or
parsley accompanied by flat bread.

WHEAT AND NUT SALAD

200g (7 ounces) fine burghul wheat
45ml (3 tablespoons) olive oil
30ml (2 tablespoons) pomegranate
concentrate
Juice of ½ a lemon
½ teaspoon cumin
½ teaspoon coriander
130g (1 cup) walnuts, chopped
130g (1 cup) hazelnuts, chopped
65g (½ cup) pine nuts, lightly toasted
½ cup parsley, chopped
Salt

1. Rinse the burghul in cold water
using a sieve. Transfer to a mixing
bowl and cover with salted water.
Leave to soak for 1 hour. Drain in
a sieve and squeeze out any excess
water.
2. Whisk the lemon juice and
pomegranate concentrate together in
a serving bowl. Gradually whisk in the
oil and add the cumin, coriander.
Finally, add the wheat, nuts and
parsley to the bowl and mix well so
that it is completely covered. Leave
to stand for at least 2 hours before
serving cold.

WHEAT AND CUCUMBER SALAD

2 bouquets parsley
1 onion, finely chopped
1 large cucumber, peeled and
finely chopped
Juice of 2 lemons
125ml (½ cup) olive oil
200g (7 ounces) fine burghul wheat
½ teaspoon dried mint
Romaine lettuce leaves or baby gems
Salt

1. Wash and rinse the parsley. Discard
the stalks and finely chop the leaves.
Place the onion in a bowl, salt and
leave to stand. Peel and finely chop
the cucumber. Place in a bowl with
the parsley.

2. Rinse the burghul wheat using a
sieve. Leave to soak in a bowl with the
lemon juice and oil.
3. Mix all the ingredients together for
no more than 5 minutes before
serving. Serve with romaine lettuce
leaves or baby gems.

COLD FISH WITH LEMON AND PINE NUTS

900g (2 pounds) white fish fillets
1 flat bread
130g (1 cup) pine nuts
Juice of 2 lemons
1 garlic clove
30ml (2 tablespoons) mild olive oil
30ml (2 tablespoons) extra virgin olive
oil
4 tablespoons pine nuts, toasted
Salt and pepper

1. Poach the fish in 30ml
(2 tablespoons) of olive oil and a little
water. Leave to cool and transfer to
a serving dish. Keep the cooking
liquid aside.
2. Soak the bread in the liquid and
squeeze dry. Blend the bread with the
pine nuts, lemon juice, olive oil, salt
and pepper and 30ml (2 tablespoons)
of the liquid to make the sauce.
3. Pour the sauce over the cold fish and
garnish with parsley and toasted pine
nuts.

COLD FISH WITH WALNUTS AND GARLIC

900g (2 pounds) white fish fillets
Juice of ½ lemon
1 flat bread, hardened
130g (1 cup) walnuts chopped
2 garlic cloves, crushed
30ml (2 tablespoons) olive oil
30ml (2 tablespoons) parsley,
finely chopped
2 tablespoons walnuts, chopped
Salt and pepper

1. Poach the fish in 30ml
(2 tablespoons) of olive oil and a little
water. Leave to cool and transfer to
a serving dish. Keep the cooking
liquid aside.
2. Soak the bread in the poaching
liquid and squeeze dry. Blend the
bread with the walnuts, garlic, oil,
parsley, lemon juice and some more
liquid if necessary.
3. Pour the sauce over the cold
fish and garnish with chopped
walnuts.

SOUPS &
STEWS

*'"Swear to me first"; so he swore to
him and sold his birthright to Jacob.
Then Jacob gave Esau bread and lentil
stew, and he ate and drank, and rose
and went his way.
Thus Esau despised his birthright.'*

GENESIS 25:34

SOUPS AND STEWS

Soups and stews were daily fare in the ancient world. Unlike modern Western cuisine, where soups precede the main course and stews are less common than in previous times, these hearty 'hot pots' commonly made up the main meal of the day. Often they resembled the potages of medieval Europe, in which wheat or barley were included. In the Holy Land they were mostly made with legumes, principally lentils: an important non-meat protein source in the ancient world, it was for a potage of lentils that Jacob gave up his birthright. Cooking was done in large earthenware pots over an open fire, typically alongside bread on 'bake-stones'. This meal was eaten in a communal fashion, where the loaves of flat bread were used as utensils. In the 'Medicine of the Prophet', As Suyuti recounts how the prophet Muhammad praised the benefits of chicken soup, which he recommended for convalescents. A method of preparing soups was popularised during the Islamic period, where meat or poultry were 'boiled twice'. This involved boiling the meat for ten minutes, throwing away the liquid and covering it with fresh water, seasoning the liquid with salt and bringing it to boil again. This method was believed to be 'cleaner' as it eliminated any need to skim the liquid.

GOURD AND CINNAMON SOUP

900g (2 pounds) gourd or pumpkin
875ml (3 ½ cups) chicken stock
875ml (3 ½ cups) milk
1 tablespoon sugar
1 cinnamon stick
½ teaspoon nutmeg, ground
Salt

1. Prepare and cube the gourd or
pumpkin. Place it in a saucepan with
the stock, milk, salt, sugar, cinnamon
stick and nutmeg. Simmer for 30
minutes on a very low heat.
2. Remove the gourd or pumpkin and
blend into a puree. Return the puree
to the pan and mix
well. Bring to the
boil again, reduce
heat and cook
for another
10 minutes.

QUINCE AND MEAT STEW

300g (10 ½ ounces) lean lamb or beef
225g (½ pound) soup bones
1.75 litres (7 cups) water
1 dried lime
30g (2 tablespoon) clarified butter
1 large onion, finely chopped
2 teaspoons saffron
1 cup quince, chopped
15ml (1 tablespoon) honey
Juice of ½ a lemon
Salt and pepper

1. Cube the meat into bite-sized pieces
and boil for 10 minutes. Remove and
throw away the liquid.
2. Transfer the meat to a large pan
with the bones and dried lime.
Cover with fresh water, season with
salt and pepper, bring slowly to boil,
reduce heat and leave to simmer
for 2 hours.
3. Fry the onion with the butter, stir
in the saffron and cook until golden.
5. Peel and chop the quince, fry for 10
minutes with the onions and add the
mixture to the soup.
6. Leave to cook for another 10
minutes. Add the honey and lemon
to taste and remove the bones if
preferred. Serve hot with rice.

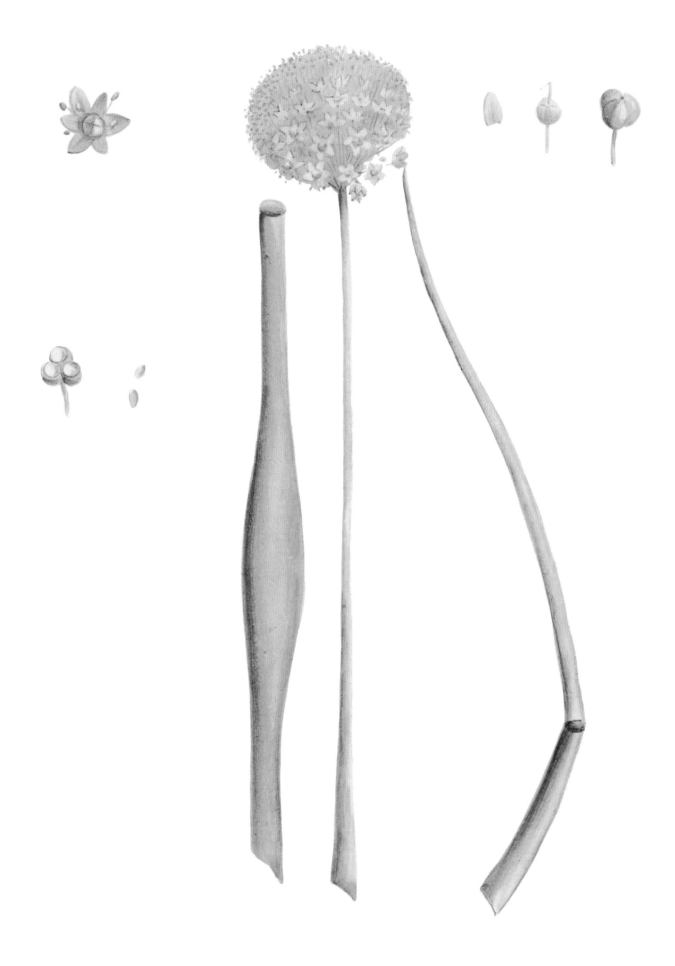

ONION

'It has been related from Muawiyya that the Prophet, may Allah bless him and grant him peace, offered food seasoned with onions to some delegates and said, "Eat of this seasoning and say, Whoever does not eat of this seasoning, or whatever else diffuses the odour of the earth, will experience harm from its waters and will suffer injury."' SAYING OF MUHAMMAD RELATED BY MUAWIYYA, IN AS SUYUTI

There has been a certain amount of discrepancy in the attitude towards onions throughout history. The prophet Muhammad praised the vegetable, yet it is reported that he himself disliked its smell. Indeed many priests and aristocrats scorned its odour, which was sometimes even associated with poverty. *Allium cepa* descends from the wild onion of Central Asia. Onions have been cultivated in Egypt for over 5000 years, where it was believed that they symbolised the universe. Egyptian cosmology interpreted the different spheres of heaven, earth and hell as concentric – similar to the layers of an onion bulb – explaining why representations of onions have been found in tombs and on inscriptions. Onions are said to have been enjoyed in Sumeria and later in Greece. They were a popular food among the plebians but were generally avoided by the Roman elite. Despite the fact that he found their odour disagreeable, Muhammad appreciated onions, which were even said to be amongst the foods in his last meal. The smell of onions on the breath can be neutralised if they are eaten with fresh parsley.

ONION SOUP

3 medium onions, chopped
60g (4 tablespoons) clarified butter
30g (2 tablespoons) plain flour
65g (½ cup) walnuts, finely chopped
1 teaspoon saffron
1 ¼ litres (5 cups) water

60ml (¼ cup) lemon juice
1 teaspoon honey
½ teaspoon dried mint, crushed
½ teaspoon cinnamon
4 eggs
Salt and pepper

1. Gently fry two of the onions in 3 tablespoons of butter until soft. Stir in the flour and cook until golden.
2. Add the walnuts and half of the saffron and stir over the heat for about 2 minutes. Stir in the water and cook until the mixture thickens. Cover and simmer for 30 minutes.
3. Add the lemon juice, honey and season with salt and pepper to taste. Cover and simmer for 15 minutes.
4. Heat the rest of the butter in a separate pan, stir in the rest of the saffron, then add the mint, cinnamon and some pepper. Remove from heat, add the mixture to the soup and blend.
5. Break each egg into a cup and slowly tip into the soup. Gently poach the eggs in the soup.
6. Divide the soup into serving bowls, allowing one egg per person. Garnish with the reserved onions and eat with flat bread.

KISHK SOUP

200g (7 ounces) beef or lamb, minced
1 small onion, finely chopped
1 clove garlic
1 cup kishk
1 ¼ litres (5 cups) water
Salt
Flat bread, to serve

1. Dry fry the meat in a saucepan for several minutes, add the onions and garlic and cook until the onions are soft, stirring occasionally.
2. Add the kishk and water, bring the soup to boil, stirring occasionally. Lower the heat and simmer for 15 minutes. Serve hot with toasted flat bread.

KISHK

At harvest time each year, burghul was soaked in yogurt in large trays over several days. It was rubbed every morning until the yogurt was absorbed, then left in the sun to dry and rubbed again to form a fine powder: kishk. The powder was then stored through the winter. To this day it is eaten for breakfast or in soups in the Levant.

KEFTA SOUP

450g (1 pound) lamb, minced
2 leeks, chopped
½ cup parsley, chopped
1 onion, finely chopped
100g (3 ½ ounces) asparagus, chopped
100g (½ cup) rice
15g (1 tablespoon) clarified butter
Salt and pepper

1. Season the meat with salt and pepper and mould into walnut-sized balls. Fry the meat balls with the butter until brown, add the onion and cook until soft.

2. Place the kefta and onion in a saucepan with the chopped vegetables. Cover with water and bring to the boil. Cover the pan, reduce heat and cook for 1 hour. Serve hot.

YOGURT SOUP

1 litre (4 cups) yogurt
1 litre (4 cups) water
100g (½ cup) rice, soaked overnight
1 egg
Salt
Dry mint

1. Combine the yogurt and water in a heavy-based saucepan.
2. Drain rice, mix with the egg, add to the yogurt and season with salt.
3. Cook over a medium heat, stirring continuously in one direction with a wooden spoon. Bring to the boil without letting it burn. Lower heat and simmer gently for 20 minutes. Serve hot or cold with a dusting of mint.

CUCUMBER AND YOGURT COLD SOUP

500ml (2 cups) yogurt
1 cucumber, peeled
½ teaspoon dried mint

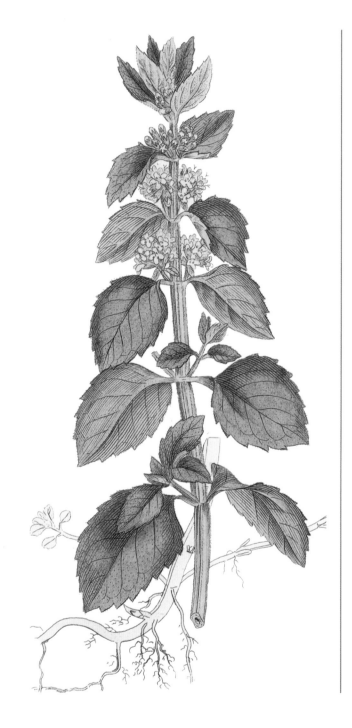

500ml (2 cups) iced water
Salt

1. Whisk the water and the yogurt together in a serving bowl. Add the mint, season with salt and mix well.
2. Peel the cucumber and cut into tiny cubes, add to the yogurt, stir and serve very cold.

LABANEYEH

450g (1 pound) spinach
1 onion, finely chopped
30ml (2 tablespoons) olive oil
1 garlic clove, crushed
1 litre (4 cups) chicken or vegetable stock
4 scallions, finely chopped
100g (½ cup) rice
500ml (2 cups) yogurt, beaten
2 teaspoons dried mint
Salt and pepper

1. Rinse the spinach and drain well using a sieve. Rinse the rice in a sieve.
2. Fry the onion in a pan with some oil until soft and add the spinach.
3. Cover the spinach with stock, add the rice, scallions and garlic. Season with salt and pepper and simmer for 20 minutes.
4. Mix in the yogurt and the mint and adjust seasoning. Keep warm without letting the mixture boil over.

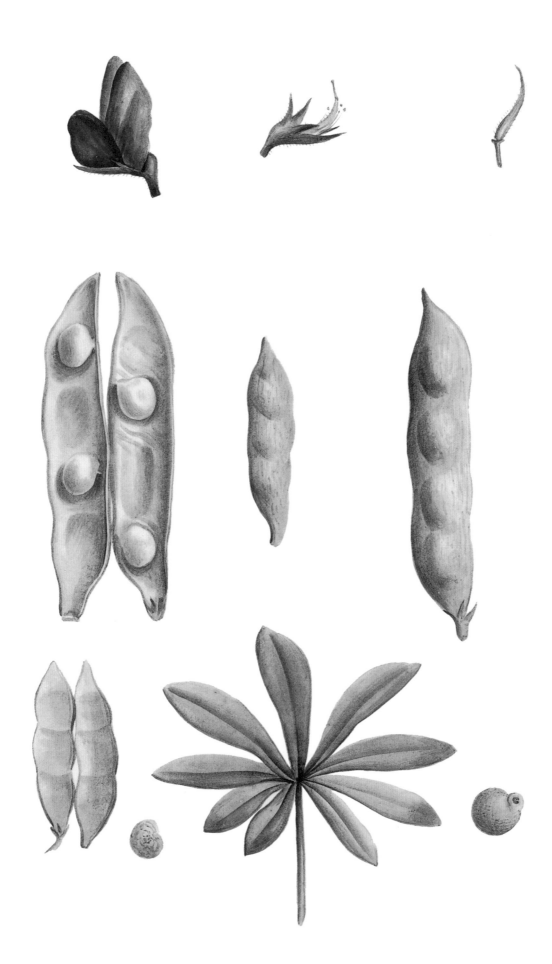

PEA

Pisum sativum were first cultivated about 8000 BC in the Eastern Mediterranean. From there they spread to India and later to China. Popular with the ancient Greeks and Romans, it was the latter that introduced them to Great Britain. Although peas are not specifically referred to in the spiritual texts, it is thought they were often mistakenly classed as beans and even lentils. Peas were mostly dried in the ancient world where they were kept through the winter. They were commonly employed as a nutritious ingredient in soups, as they are made up of twenty-three per cent protein. The pods of green peas are inedible, though certain cultivars such as *mangetout* can be eaten in their entirety. Although green peas are commonly canned or eaten fresh in Europe and North America, eighty per cent of the world's peas are grown in Russia and China and are actually dried.

PEA SOUP

450g (1 pound) garden peas
2 leeks, chopped
30ml (2 tablespoons) olive oil
1 litre (4 cups) chicken stock
1 teaspoon mint, dried
Salt and pepper

1. Sweat the leeks in a large pot with the olive oil until transparent, season with salt.
2. Add the peas and leave to cook for several minutes.
3. Cover with chicken stock and leave to simmer until the vegetables are tender.
4. Puree the soup and season with salt, pepper and mint. Serve hot.

GRAIN

'When you reap your harvest
in your field, and have forgotten a sheaf
in the field, you shall not go back
to get it; it shall be for the sojourner,
the fatherless, and the widow; that the
Lord your God may bless you in all
the work of your hands.'

DEUTERONOMY 24:19

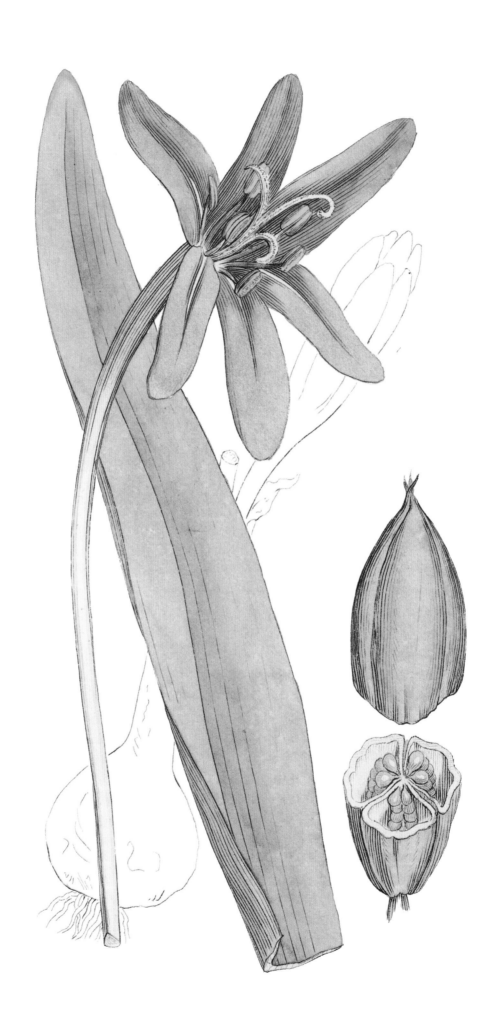

GRAIN

Grain has been the principal staple in the Near East since prehistoric times. Root staples such as the potato arrived only after the discovery of the Americas. Grain continues to make up the bulk of the Levantine diet, supplemented by vegetables, fruit and small amounts of dairy produce, fish and meat. Modern research indicates that a diet based heavily on grain, such as that of the Near East, results in fewer instances of coronary disease and cancer. This remains the case in many developing countries where people do not consume as much meat, potatoes and dairy produce as in the Western world.

Archaeological records show that nomads in the Fertile Crescent began to gather wild cereal grasses, such as einkorn and emmer wheat, as early as 9000 years ago. The domestication of these cereal grasses heralded the beginning of farming. By the time of Abraham, cereals and legumes had been cultivated in the 'Cradle of Civilization', for over 5000 years. The whole produce of the field is referred to as 'corn' throughout the spiritual texts but bears no relation to American maize.

Although grain was sometimes plucked from the field and eaten raw, as it was by Jesus and his apostles [MATTHEW 12:1], it is difficult to digest in its raw state. Normally the ripe cereal was harvested and then threshed with animals or sticks to separate the wheat from the chaff. Grain was stored whole, as once the oil within the kernels is exposed to light and oxygen it quickly turns rancid. It was ground as needed using a hand-operated millstone, which would later be driven by animals such as oxen.

The vast majority of grains were ground into flour to make bread, the mainstay of these ancient people. However, grains were also prepared in other ways. Grain could be eaten 'parched' [1 SAMUEL 25:18] by toasting ears of corn and other cereals over a fire [RUTH 2:14] or parboiled and cracked to make 'burghul'. The many rules in the Bible that relate to how best to cut, thresh and distribute cereal crops corroborate their importance in society. Punishments were laid out for stealing 'corn' from fields, as were guidelines indicating that some cereals were so important that some should be left in the fields to ensure poorer people got their share.

WHEAT

'And when they had eaten enough, they lightened the ship, and cast out the wheat into the sea.' ACTS 27:38

The domestication of wild wheat grasses, such as emmer and einkorn, over ten thousand years ago in the Fertile Crescent signalled the end of nomadic life and the formation of settled civilizations in the Holy Land. Wheat and barley were first farmed along the hilly flanks of South West Asia. Evidence of grains in various states, dating back to about 8000 BC, has been found at sites in the Jordan valley, Jericho and Tell Aswad. Wheat was the most prized Levantine crop. It is mentioned as the grain of choice from which to make bread throughout the Old Testament and remains the world's most widely produced crop to this day. It is often erroneously referred to as 'corn' rather than specifically as wheat in the spiritual texts, but is also specially mentioned [EXODUS 9:32]. As the preferred grain, it was offered up to deities; to Osiris by the Egyptians and to Yahweh by the Hebrews. There was a great demand for wheat in Rome. The Romans imported wheat from all over the empire, from Britain to the Levant, and even set up an official to manage the 'corn' supply known as the *Praefectus annonae*.

MEAT AND WHEAT PUREE

This dish is akin to tharid, a favourite of Muhammad. The slow cooking process renders the wheat as a puree and the meat falls away from the bone. This dish would have also been prepared with the affordable barley. Chopped vegetables such as carrots and courgettes can be included in this dish and should be added to the pan during the last hour of cooking.

450g (1 pound) lamb on the bone
200g (7 ounces) wheat or barley
Salt

1. Boil the meat in water for 10 minutes. Remove and throw away the liquid.
2. Place the meat in a saucepan with the wheat and cover with fresh water and season with salt.
3. Bring to the boil, reduce heat, cover and simmer for at least 5 hours. Stir occasionally and serve hot.

BURGHUL

'Crush a fool in a mortar with a pestle along with crushed grain but the folly will not be driven out.' PROVERBS 27:22

Often known as bulgar or bulghur wheat, burghul was a common Levantine way of preparing wheat. The process of making burghul seems to have emerged in ancient Assyria. The wheat was slowly boiled in order to separate the chaff from the grain and parched in the heat of the sun so that it became hard. Finally, it was ground using a pestle and mortar as described in proverbs [PROVERBS 27:22]. Burghul was boiled or steamed with vegetables and meat and often served accompanied by yogurt. By quickly frying the burghul before and after boiling, the grains retain a hard texture which complements their nutty flavour. Today there are three types of burghul on the market: coarse, medium and fine. They can be purchased in Middle Eastern stores and, increasingly, in Western supermarkets.

BURGHUL WITH RAISINS AND PINE NUTS

875ml (3 ½ cups) chicken stock
400g (2 cups) coarse burghul
65g (½ cup) pine nuts
60g (4 tablespoons) clarified butter
30g (¼ cup) raisins (optional)
Salt and pepper

1. Leave the raisins to soak in cold water for 20 minutes. Rinse and drain the burghul wheat using a sieve. Press out any excess water. Heat 15g (1 tablespoon) of the butter in a frying pan. Fry the burghul, stirring constantly until it is coated and dry.
2. Transfer to a saucepan with boiling stock. Bring to the boil, reduce heat and cook until the burghul absorbs all the liquid, about 15 minutes.
3. Fry the pine nuts in the remainder of the butter until golden. Transfer the burghul to the frying pan, mix with the pine nuts, stir in the drained raisins and season with salt and pepper. Cook until all the liquid has evaporated.

POMEGRANATE AND WALNUT BURGHUL

400g (2 cups) burghul
875ml (3 ½ cups) chicken stock
70ml (¼ cup) pomegranate concentrate

1 onion, finely chopped
70g (½ cup) walnuts, chopped
45g (3 tablespoons) clarified butter
Salt and pepper

1. Rinse and drain the burghul wheat using a sieve. Press out any excess water. Heat 15g (1 tablespoon) of the butter in a frying pan. Fry the burghul, stirring constantly until it is coated and dry.
2. Transfer to a saucepan with the boiling stock. Bring to the boil, reduce heat and cook until the burghul absorbs all the liquid, about 15 minutes.
3. Gently fry the onion in the remaining butter. Add the walnuts and pomegranate concentrate to the frying pan and cook for 5 minutes. Transfer the burghul to the pan, mix with the sauce and make sure any excess liquid has evaporated. Season with salt and pepper, serve hot.

BURGHUL AND VEGETABLES

400g (2 cups) burghul
15g (1 tablespoon) clarified butter
875ml (3 ½ cups) chicken stock
2 zucchini, peeled and diced
1 carrot, diced
Salt and pepper

1. Rinse and drain the burghul wheat using a sieve. Press out any excess water.

Heat 15g (1 tablespoon) of the butter in a frying pan. Fry the burghul, stirring constantly until it is coated and dry.
2. Place the grains in a saucepan with the diced vegetables and cover with the chicken stock. Bring to the boil, reduce heat and cook until the burghul has absorbed the liquid and the vegetables are tender. Season with salt and pepper. Serve hot.

BURGHUL WITH LENTILS

400g (2 cups) burghul
15g (1 tablespoon) clarified butter
875ml (3 ½ cups) chicken stock
200g (1 cup) lentils
Salt and pepper

1. Rinse and drain the burghul wheat using a sieve. Press out any excess water. Heat 15g (1 tablespoon) of the butter in a frying pan. Fry the burghul, stirring constantly until it is coated and dry.
2. Rinse the lentils and place them in a saucepan with the burghul, cover with boiling stock. Bring to the boil, reduce heat and cook until both the burghul and lentils are tender. Season with salt and pepper. Serve hot.

MILLET

'And you, take wheat and barley, beans and lentils, millet and spelt, and put them into a single vessel, and make bread of them.' EZEKIEL 4:9

Millet has been an appellation for numerous grains throughout history but it is certain that *Panicum milliaceum* was eaten in the Holy Land. Known as *dokhan* by the Hebrews and *kenkhros* by the Greeks, it was cultivated all over the ancient world. While the stalks were fed to cattle, the seeds were made into porridge or gruel and were combined with other grains to make bread. Herodotus described six-foot-high millet in the Hanging Gardens of Babylon. It has been suggested that the millet referred to in Ezekiel was possibly sorghum, a millet-like grain that is still a staple food in parts of Africa. Millet is still a staple in parts of Asia such as Nepal, but had, however, been largely forgotten in the West until it was re-discovered by health food enthusiasts and vegetarians in recent years. In fact, millet is known to be an excellent source of protein and is a good alternative grain for those who follow a gluten-free diet.

MILLET AND VEGETABLE PORRIDGE

200g (1 cup) millet
1 carrot, chopped
1 zucchini
200g (7 ounces) gourd or pumpkin, chopped
1 onion
30ml (2 tablespoons) olive oil
2 tablespoons parsley, chopped
Salt and pepper

1. Heat the oil in a pan, gently cook the onion until soft, add the chopped gourd, carrot and courgette and cook for 2 minutes.
2. Toast the grains in a separate pan for 2 minutes, stirring continuously.
3. Place the grains in a saucepan with the vegetables and cover with hot water.
4. Season with salt. Bring to the boil, reduce heat and leave to cook for 30 minutes or until the grains have absorbed the water.
5. Serve hot garnished with parsley.

MILLET AND SESAME BAKE

200g (1 cup) millet
750ml (3 cups) water
30ml (2 tablespoons) sesame oil
2 carrots, chopped
1 onion, finely chopped
1 garlic clove
1 teaspoon dill
1 teaspoon thyme
125g (½ cup) sesame seeds
3 tablespoons flour
Salt and pepper
Yogurt, to serve

1. Rinse the grains, transfer to a pan
and cover with boiling water. Season
with salt and bring to the boil. Reduce
heat and leave to cook for 30 minutes
or until the grains have soaked up all
the water.
2. Fry the onion in the oil until soft,
add the carrot and garlic and cook for
5 minutes.
3. Toast the sesame seeds in a
separate pan.
4. Transfer the cooked millet, semi-
cooked vegetables and toasted sesame
seeds to a mixing bowl and combine
the ingredients.
5. Place the mixture in a shallow oven
dish and cook in a pre-heated oven at
200C (400F) for 1 hour. Serve hot or
cold with yogurt.

RICE

'The master of your food is meat, and rice comes next.' SAYING OF MUHAMMAD
RELATED BY AS SUYUTI

Wild rice strains emerged during the Cretaceous period, millions of years ago. *Oryza sativa* was first cultivated around 3000 BC in China. Rice most likely arrived in the Middle East via Persia about 1000 BC: the Hebrews were introduced to it during the Babylonian captivity. Alexander the Great came across the grain during his Persian expedition and later it was a luxury import in Rome. The English word rice and the Arabic *rouz* derive from the Aramaic (the language spoken by Jesus) name for the grain, *ourouzza*. By the end of the first century BC, Levantine farmers grew enough rice for it to become an export crop. It had become established as a foodstuff among the urban elite during the Byzantine period and rice cooked in clarified butter is said to have been savoured by the prophet Muhammad. Consumers tend to favour milled rice and therefore the bran, as well as the husk, is also removed from most rice. Unfortunately, the B vitamins and fibre content are lost during the milling process. Rice can also be ground into flour and fermented to make vinegar or alcohol. As the world's most important staple grain, it can support twice as many people per acre than wheat but lacks the essential fibre; unbalanced rice-based diets can result in conditions such as beri beri. Rice is easy to digest and can be flavoured and coloured with spices. The most refined rice in the Middle East is said to come from Persia, where there are numerous delicate long-grain varieties.

RICE WITH HERBS

400g (2 cups) basmati rice
Large bunch of mixed herbs such
as tarragon, chives, flat-leaf
parsley, coriander and dill, all
finely chopped

6 scallions, finely chopped
30ml (2 tablespoons) clarified butter
Salt

1. Wash and rinse the rice in a sieve. Drain and transfer to a saucepan of boiling water. Bring to the boil,

reduce heat and cook until tender.

2. Add the herbs and scallions to the rice and drain using a sieve.

3. Gently melt the butter in the pan. Return the rice to the pan, season with salt and stir carefully. Cover the pan with a cloth and secure with a tightly fitting lid. Leave to steam for 20 minutes on a very low heat. Serve hot.

RICE WITH PINE NUTS AND RAISINS

1 large onion, chopped
30ml (2 tablespoons) oil
130g (1 cup) pine nuts
400g (2 cups) basmati rice, washed and rinsed
750ml (3 cups) chicken or vegetable stock, warmed
1 teaspoon cinnamon
2 tablespoons raisins
60g (4 tablespoons) clarified butter
Salt and pepper

1. Fry the onion in a little of the butter until transparent. Add the pine nuts and cook until golden.

2. Add the rice and stir until all the grains are coated in the fat.

3. Cover with the stock, stir in the rice, cinnamon, currants and season with salt and pepper. Bring to the boil, lower heat, cover and gently simmer for 20 minutes or until the rice is cooked.

4. Remove from heat, gently stir in the rest of the butter and serve hot.

RICE WITH DATES

400g (2 cups) basmati rice
45g (3 tablespoons) clarified butter
170g (⅔ cup) dates, chopped
140g (1 cup) almonds, chopped

1. Rinse the rice using a sieve. Fry the almonds in 2 tablespoons of butter until golden. Stir in the dried fruit and keep over a medium heat for 10 minutes, stirring continuously.

2. Place the rice in a saucepan of boiling water for 10 minutes and then drain well.

3. Melt the remaining butter in a saucepan and re-introduce the rice, along with the dates and almonds. Cover the pan with a cloth and secure with a tightly fitting lid. Leave to steam on an extremely low heat for 20 minutes or until the rice is light and fluffy.

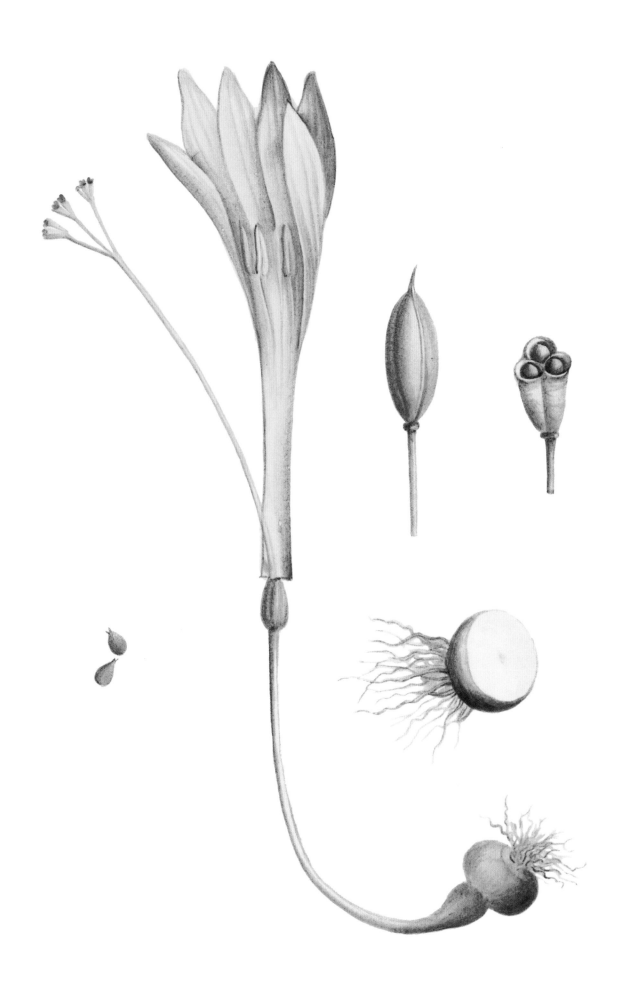

SAFFRON

'Your channel is an orchard of pomegranates with all the choicest fruits, henna with nard, nard with saffron.' SONG OF SOLOMON 4:13–14

The dried stigmas of the *Crocus sativa* produce the world's most expensive spice. Cultivated in the Levant since ancient times, saffron was used to dye clothes, as a medicine and to colour and perfume food. The stigma must be hand-picked and the plants must be uprooted after three years. Owing to its high price saffron has been substituted with lesser yet more affordable spices, such as turmeric and safflower. Although these substitutes colour the food, they lack the hypnotic fragrance of saffron. The word saffron is originally from the Arabic *zaffran* – 'to be yellow'. As Suyuti said that saffron fortifies the essence of the soul and could have an aphrodisiac effect. It was therefore forbidden during the month of Muharram. Saffron is an essential ingredient in Middle Eastern festive rice dishes and the Spanish dish *paella*, which is said to be heavily influenced by the Moors.

SAFFRON RICE

400g (2 cups) basmati rice
¼ teaspoon saffron
130g (1 cup) almonds chopped
130g (1 cup) pine nuts
½ teaspoon cinnamon
60g (4 tablespoons) clarified butter
Salt

1. Rinse the rice using a sieve. Transfer it to a bowl with the saffron, cover with water, stir and leave to soak for 1 hour.
2. Drain the rice and save the liquid. Transfer the liquid into a saucepan and bring to the boil with salt. Add the rice, cinnamon and season. Reduce to a low heat, cover with a cloth and secure the lid with a weight.
3. Cook on a very low heat until the rice is light and fluffy.
3. Fry the almonds and pine nuts in the butter. Pour the nut-infused butter into the rice and mix carefully. Transfer to a serving dish and decorate with the nuts.

PERFUMED SAFFRON RICE

400g (2 cups) basmati rice
750ml (3 cups) chicken stock
1 teaspoon cardamom seeds
2 cloves
2 cinnamon sticks
¼ teaspoon saffron
65g (½ cup) almonds, chopped
Salt and pepper

1. Rinse the rice using a sieve.
Bring the stock to the boil and simmer
with the cardamom, cloves and
cinnamon for several minutes.
2. Add the saffron, rice and season,
bring to the boil again. Lower heat and
simmer for about 20 minutes. Serve
garnished with chopped almonds.

RICE WITH SPINACH

450g (1 pound) fresh spinach
1 large onion, chopped
15ml (1 tablespoon) oil
400g (2 cups) basmati rice
750ml (3 cups) chicken or vegetable
stock
½ teaspoon nutmeg
Salt and pepper

1. Wash the spinach, drain well and
chop finely.
2. Fry the onion in the oil until soft.
Add the rice and stir until all the grains
are coated.
3. Cover with stock and bring to the
boil. Reduce the heat and season with
salt.
4. Add the spinach, stir and cook over
a very low heat for about 20 minutes
or until the rice is cooked. Season with
nutmeg, salt and pepper and serve hot
accompanied by yogurt.

RICE WITH LENTILS

300g (1 ½ cups) rice
200g (1 cup) red lentils
2 garlic cloves, crushed
2 onions, finely sliced
1 teaspoon cinnamon
90g (6 tablespoons) clarified butter
Salt and pepper

1. Rinse the lentils using a sieve.
Place in a saucepan and cover with
water. Bring to the boil, reduce heat
and leave to cook for 45 minutes on a
medium heat.
2. Rinse the rice, again using a sieve,
and add to the pan with the lentils,
leave to cook for another 20 minutes
or until all the liquid has evaporated
3. Heat the butter in a pan and fry the
onion slices until blackened. Transfer
the onions and remaining butter
(optional) to the lentil and rice
mixture. Serve hot with yogurt.

RICE WITH GOURD

450g (1 pound) gourd or pumpkin
1 onion, chopped
30ml (2 tablespoons) oil
400g (2 cups) basmati rice
750ml (3 cups) chicken or
vegetable stock
5 cardamom pods
1 ½ teaspoons cinnamon
2 tablespoons tarragon, chopped
30ml (2 tablespoons) clarified butter
Salt and pepper

1. Rinse the rice using a sieve. Prepare
and cube the pumpkin.
2. Fry the onion in some oil until
golden. Add the rinsed and drained
rice and stir until the grains are coated
in fat.
3. Add the cubed pumpkin and cook
for several minutes. Cover
with stock.
4. Stir in the spices and season with salt
and pepper. Bring to the boil and add
the rice. Bring to the boil again,
reduce heat, cover and simmer for 20
minutes or until the rice and pumpkin
are tender.
5. Remove from heat. Gently stir in
the butter and tarragon. Place a cloth
on the pan and secure with a
tight-fitting lid and leave to
stand for 10 minutes.
Adjust seasonings, fork
gently and serve hot.

MAKLOUBA

200g (7 ounces) aubergine
400g (2 cups) rice
300g (10 ½ ounces) minced lamb
200g (7 ounces) cubed lamb
75g (5 tablespoons) clarified butter
130g (1 cup) pine nuts
130g (1 cup) almonds
Salt and pepper

The aubergines in this dish can be
replaced with desert truffles (*kama* in
Arabic). They are less pungent and
cheaper than the European variety.

1. Fry the pine nuts and almonds in
4 tablespoons of the butter and set
aside. Dry fry the lamb until browned
and season with salt and pepper.
2. Peel the aubergines and cut into
strips. Rinse the rice in a sieve.
3. Melt the remaining butter in a
saucepan and swirl it around so that it
coats the bottom and the sides. Spoon
a layer of rice into the saucepan
followed by a layer of aubergine and
so on. Cover with hot water and
season. Bring to the boil, reduce to
a very low heat and cook for 45
minutes.
4. When cooked, carefully turn the
contents on to a serving dish. Lay the
meat over the mound and decorate
with the fried nuts and the nut-infused
clarified butter. Serve hot.

VEGETABLES

'And God said, "Behold, I have
given you every plant yielding seed
which is upon the face of all
the earth, and every tree with seed in
its fruit; you shall have them
for food; I have given every green
plant for food."'

GENESIS I : 29–30

VEGETABLES

'Better a dinner of vegetables where love is, than a fatted ox and hatred therewith.'
PROVERBS 15:17

References such as the one above, throughout the Pentateuch, suggest that God originally intended man's diet to be based on vegetables. Plants are the first food mentioned in the book of Genesis and it is only after the flood that man is reluctantly permitted to eat flesh. Furthermore, where meat eating is proscribed, temperance is encouraged. Although vegetables were not the preferred food in the ancient world, they were nevertheless appreciated and certainly accounted for the better part of the typical Holy Lander's diet. Ahab's burning desire to appropriate Naboth's vineyard so that he could convert it into a vegetable garden [KINGS 21:1] illustrates that vegetables were held in some esteem, especially during times of hunger. Vegetables were the food most readily available in the the Holy Land, and with the exception of fishing communities, meat was reserved for feasts and the very wealthy. Modern research tells us that a diet based primarily on vegetables, such as that of the Holy Landers, promotes good health, vitality and longevity. Vegetables are packed with a plethora of vitamins and minerals; when they comprise the better part of a diet they can help prevent heart disease, high cholesterol, cancer and obesity. Recently many have begun to question how our vegetables and fruit are grown. Today, in the developed world, there is increasing resistance to the use of chemicals and genetic modification in growing vegetables. The concerned cook should use organically grown vegetables, yet these products remain expensive and often unobtainable.

GOURDS & MARROWS

'Jonah was also sent with a message. He fled to the laden ship, cast lots, and was condemned. The whale swallowed him, for he had sinned; and had he not devoutly praised the Lord he would have stayed in its belly till the Day of Resurrection. We threw him, gravely ill, upon a desolate shore and caused a gourd tree to grow over him.' QURAN, THE RANKS 37:130–148

The Quran and the Bible both recount how the Lord sent a bush to shelter Jonah after he was expelled from the mouth of the whale; the St. James version of Bible specifies that this was a gourd bush. The genus *Curcurbita* encompasses gourds, squashes, marrows and zucchini, making classification of this family somewhat haphazard in history and translations. The pumpkin mentioned in this Hadith was most probably a gourd, as the sweeter and more palatable *Curcurbita pepo* developed in the Americas. There are some recipes in this book for gourd but since it is often unavailable, they have been designed to work just as well with pumpkin and most kinds of squash.

Cucurbits are versatile vegetables that can be used in both savoury and sweet dishes. Muhammad is reported to have been so fond of these vegetables that when he was presented with a bowl of meat and pumpkin soup, he selected the pieces of pumpkin before eating the meat. Gourd is often given to convalescents and children as it is nutritious and easy to digest. Zucchini, the young cuttings of a type of marrow, *Cucurbita pepo*, called courgettes in Britain after the French *courgettes d'Italie,* are very popular in modern cuisine. As Suyuti mentioned that marrows were pre-scribed to the sick and convalescents; they remain important winter vegetables in the Near East, where they are often stuffed.

'The Prophet Muhammad, may Allah bless him and grant him peace, was very fond of dried pumpkin. He once said, "Let them have pumpkins, for they stimulate the intellect and the brain."' SAYING OF MUHAMMAD, RELATED BY AL BUKHARI

'The Lord appointed a bush, and made it come up over Jonah, to give shade over his head, to save him from his discomfort; so Jonah was very happy about the bush.'
JONAH 4:6

JONAH'S GOURD MASH

900g (2 pounds) gourd
60ml (4 tablespoons) olive oil
30ml (2 tablespoons) wine vinegar
15ml (1 tablespoon) honey
1 clove garlic, crushed

1. Peel and dice the gourd.
2. Place the crushed garlic in a pan with 2 tablespoons of olive oil and gently colour. Add the chopped gourd and cover with water.
3. Cover and leave to cook for 15 minutes or until tender.
4. Stir in the honey, olive oil and remainder of the vinegar. Serve cold.

GOURD AND SESAME MASH

900g (2 pounds) gourd
125ml (½ cup) lemon juice
125ml (½ cup) sesame seed paste
2 tablespoons parsley, chopped
30ml (2 tablespoons) olive oil
Salt

1. Peel and dice the gourd. Place in a saucepan of salted water, bring to the boil and cook on a medium heat for 40 minutes or until tender.
2. Remove from the pan, drain and mash the gourd in a mixing bowl.
3. Whisk the lemon juice and sesame seed paste together and season with salt. Add to the pumpkin. Sprinkle with chopped parsley and drizzle with olive oil. Serve hot or cold.

STUFFED CALABASH GOURD

450g (1 pound) calabash or bottle gourd
200g (7 ounces) rice
200g (7 ounces) lamb, minced
1 teaspoon saffron, crushed
1 teaspoon cumin
Juice of 2 lemons
30ml (2 tablespoons) sesame seed paste
1 tablespoon dried mint
Salt

1. Wash the rice and mix with the minced lamb, saffron, cumin and salt in a bowl with a cup of water. Leave to absorb for 30 minutes.
2. Prepare the calabash by emptying it of all its seeds and fibrous material. Stuff the vegetable, up to 2cm from the top, with the lamb and rice mixture.

3. Place the stuffed gourd in a saucepan and cover with water. Secure the lid with a weight. Cook on medium heat for 1 hour or until well done.

4. Whisk the sesame seed paste and lemon together to make a white sauce. Add 2 cups of water and the mint. Pour the sauce over the gourd and leave to cook for another 10 minutes. Transfer to a dish and serve hot.

STUFFED GOURD ALEPPO STYLE

1 large gourd or pumpkin
Oil, to fry
100g (¾ cup) pine nuts
45g (3 tablespoons) clarified butter
450g (1 pound) lamb, minced
1 cup parsley, chopped
125ml (½ cup) pomegranate concentrate
500ml (2 cups) yogurt

1. Peel and slice the pumpkin along its ridges so that it is in several rectangular pieces. Quarter these, then using a corer make a cavity the size of your index finger in each piece. Fry each piece in a little oil until golden.

2. Fry the pine nuts with clarified butter in a separate pan. Set aside and brown the meat in the nut-infused butter. Re-introduce the pine nuts to the pan, mix in the parsley and season.

3. Stuff the pieces of pumpkin with the meat mixture.

4. Place the pumpkin pieces in a saucepan, cover with the pomegranate concentrate and water. Season with salt and pepper and cook on a medium heat for 1 hour.

5. Pour the yogurt over the hot pieces of pumpkin and serve immediately with rice. Season with salt and pepper.

EBLA ZUCCHINI

900g (2 pounds) small zucchini
450g (1 pound) lamb, minced
1 cup parsley, chopped
100g (¾ cup) pine nuts
500ml (2 cups) yogurt
45g (3 tablespoons) clarified butter

1. Peel and core the zucchini. Fry briefly in well-heated oil.

2. Fry the pine nuts with clarified butter in a separate pan. Set the pine nuts aside and brown the meat in the nut-infused butter. Re-introduce the pine nuts, mix in the parsley and season.

3. Stuff the zucchini with the meat mixture and lay them out in an oven dish. Cover with 250ml (1 cup) of salted water and bake at 200C (400F) for 1 hour. Season well.

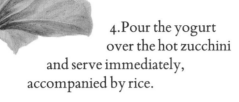

4.Pour the yogurt over the hot zucchini and serve immediately, accompanied by rice.

STUFFED POMEGRANATE ZUCCHINI

450g (1 pound) zucchini
200g (7 ounces) lamb, minced
45g (3 tablespoons) clarified butter
65g (½ cup) pine nuts
1 onion, chopped
Juice of ½ lemon
125ml (½ cup) pomegranate concentrate
Salt

1. Peel and core the zucchini.
2. Gently fry the meat, pine nuts and onion in the clarified butter for about 10 minutes.
3. Stuff the mixture into the zucchini and lay them out in an oven dish. Cover with water and lemon juice and season with salt and pepper.
4. Cover the dish with a secure lid. Bake in a pre-heated oven at 250C (500F) for 1 hour 15 minutes. Add pomegranate concentrate 5 minutes before the end, then serve hot.

VEGETARIAN STUFFING

200g (4 cups) rice
2 onions, chopped
65g (½ cup) pine nuts
125ml (½ cup) pomegranate concentrate
60ml (4 tablespoons) clarified butter
Salt and pepper

1. Gently fry the onion with half of the clarified butter until soft. Add the rice and stir until all the grains are coated.
2. In a separate pan gently fry the pine nuts until golden. Add them to the rice, pour in the pomegranate concentrate and season with salt and pepper. Stir for a few moments over the heat and set aside to be used as vegetable stuffing.

ZUCCHINI SLICES WITH YOGURT

450g (1 pound) zucchini
250ml (1 cup) yogurt
Olive oil, to fry
Salt

1. Wash the zucchini and cut lengthways into strips.
2. Heat some oil in a pan and fry the zucchini until lightly browned. Pat dry and sprinkle with salt.
3. Serve hot with yogurt.

ZUCCHINI GRATIN

450g (1 pound) zucchini
2 scallions, finely chopped
250g (½ pound) feta cheese, crumbled
4 eggs, lightly beaten
½ teaspoon nutmeg, grated
2 teaspoons parsley, chopped
Salt and pepper

1. Wash the zucchini and slice into rounds. Cook in salted boiling water for 5 minutes, drain and transfer to a baking dish.
2. Place the crumbled feta in a bowl with the beaten eggs. Add the nutmeg, parsley, scallions and season with salt and pepper, mix well.
3. Pour the egg and cheese mixture over the zucchini. Bake in a pre-heated oven at 180C (350F) for 30 minutes until the top is coloured. Serve with yogurt.

ZUCCHINI MASH

450g (1 pound) zucchini
Juice of ½ lemon
30ml (2 tablespoons) olive oil
1 garlic clove, crushed
1 tablespoon dried mint
10 black olives, pitted
Salt and pepper

1. Peel the zucchini and dice into small pieces. Place in a pan of salted water, bring to the boil, lower heat and cook until tender. Drain, squeeze out any excess liquid, puree and transfer the zucchini to a serving bowl.
2. Mix in the lemon, oil, garlic and olives with the zucchini and season. Serve cold.

AUBERGINE

The aubergine is the only member of the *Solanaceae* or nightshade family to come from tropical Asia. The others, such as the tomato, come from tropical America. Known as 'eggplant' in the United States, the oriental white variety were thought to resemble large goose eggs. They are first thought to have been cultivated in India about 4000 years ago, where they were grown in the wild. It is most likely that the Persians first introduced *Solanum melongena* to the Levant, where it was well established by the time of Muhammad. The Moorish con-quest of the Iberian peninsula saw the aubergine spread through Southern Europe. The English word aubergine is taken directly from the French, which is derived from the Arabic word *Al badinjan*, and can be traced back to the Sanskrit. As Suyuti thought aubergine was a good vegetable to 'balance out' foods, especially the white variety. Aubergines are largely made up of water but also contain a large amount of potassium. They are rarely eaten raw but can be boiled, fried, roasted and stuffed. Their versatility makes them popular with vegetarians.

AUBERGINE SLICES WITH YOGURT

3 medium aubergines
Salt
Oil, to fry
250ml (1 cup) thick yogurt, strained
2 teaspoons parsley or mint, chopped

1. Peel the aubergines if desired and slice into rounds. Sprinkle with coarse salt and leave to stand for 30 minutes. Wipe the salt from the slices with a cloth. This procedure will ensure that the aubergine does not absorb too much oil and can be applied to all dishes where aubergines are fried.

2. Heat some oil in a pan. Fry each slice on both sides until brown and soft. Pat dry of any excess oil with a cloth.
3. Transfer to a serving dish and serve hot or cold with the yogurt and herbs.

AUBERGINES WITH YOGURT

4 medium aubergines, peeled
500ml (2 cups) yogurt
200g (7 ounces) minced lamb
Sesame oil, to fry
65g (½ cup) pine nuts
15g (1 tablespoon) clarified butter

1. Cut the aubergines lengthways into 2 pieces. Heat the oil in a pan, fry the pieces on both sides, and pat away any excess oil.
2. Gently fry the pine nuts in the butter until golden and wipe the pan of any excess oil. Place the meat in the pan and cook until brown. Return the nuts to the pan and mix with the meat.
3. Lay the aubergines out in an oven dish. Spread the meat and nut mixture on top of the aubergines and cover with 125ml (½ cup) of water.
4. Cook in a pre-heated oven at 240C (475F) for 20 minutes. Serve hot covered with the yogurt.

STUFFED AUBERGINES

12 baby aubergines
200g (1 cup) coarse burghul
90g (½ cup) chickpeas, soaked overnight
½ teaspoon coriander
15g (1 tablespoon) clarified butter
Juice of 1 lemon
Salt and pepper

1. Rinse the burghul using a sieve. Transfer to a pan and fry with the butter, stir in the chickpeas, coriander and season with the salt and pepper.
2. Cut the caps off the aubergines and core them, making the cavity as large as possible.

3. Stuff the aubergines with the burghul mixture and place them in a large saucepan. Cover with water and the lemon juice. Secure the lid of the saucepan.
4. Cook on a high heat for 30 minutes, then reduce to a medium heat and cook for a further 30 minutes. Serve hot.

AUBERGINE AND ZUCCHINI MOUSSAKA

450g (1 pound) baby aubergines, peeled
450g (1 pound) zucchini, peeled
225g (½ pound) lamb, minced
65g (½ cup) pine nuts
2 onions, finely chopped
60ml (½ cup) pomegranate concentrate, diluted to make 1 cup
30ml (2 tablespoons) olive oil
Salt and pepper

1. Slice the vegetables lengthways into strips. Heat the oil, briefly fry the slices and leave to drain.
2. Gently fry the pine nuts in some oil until golden. Remove, and fry the onion in the same nut-infused oil. Mix the pomegranate concentrate into the soft onions and stir. In a separate pan, brown the minced meat and mix it with the pine nuts.
3. Lay a bed of the aubergine at the bottom of an oven dish. Season.

SPINACH & CHARD

'They pick mallow and the leaves of bushes and to warm themselves the roots of broom' JOB 30:4

The mallow mentioned in the Bible was widely enjoyed by the ancient Greeks and Romans, who ate it in broths or salads and used it as a garnish. But by the medieval era the mucilaginous *Malus sylvestris*, applauded for its healing properties by Pliny, was seldom eaten. In the centuries following the death of Jesus, mallow was supplanted by the more palatable spinach. *Spinacea oleracea* arrived in the Levant from Persia, where it was first cultivated. Later, it was brought to Europe with the Moorish conquest. It is a nutritious plant, which contains considerable amounts of iron, calcium and vitamins C and B. As Suyuti reported that it was a good laxative. Although chard tasted very similar to spinach, the coarser *Beta vulgaris* is actually a member of the beet family. It is said to have been grown in the Hanging Gardens of Babylon and was known as *silq* to the Arabs.

Cover with a layer of the meat and pine nut mixture, followed by a layer of zucchini. Season. Top with the pomegranate onions then bake for 1 hour at 250C.

MALLOW WITH FRUIT AND NUTS

450g (1 pound) spinach
1 onion, chopped
15ml (1 tablespoon) olive oil
2 tablespoons pine nuts
1 tablespoon raisins, soaked
Salt and pepper

1. Rinse the spinach, drain in a colander and squeeze out any excess water. Place in a pan over a low heat, cover and leave to wilt.
2. Fry the chopped onion with the oil until golden. In a separate pan gently fry the pine nuts with a little oil.
3. Add the spinach, the onions and the pine nuts.
4. Add the drained raisins, season with salt and pepper and cook for another 5 minutes on a low heat. Serve hot.

SPINACH WITH WALNUTS AND POMEGRANATE

200g (7 ounces) spinach
60ml (4 tablespoons) olive oil
65g (½ cup) walnuts, chopped
2 medium onions, finely chopped
Salt
30ml (2 tablespoons) pomegranate concentrate
1 teaspoon sumac

1. Rinse the spinach in a colander, drain well and squeeze out any excess water.
2. Soften the onions in half of the oil. Add the spinach to the pan and season with salt and pepper. Cook on a low heat for about 20 minutes.
3. Stir in the pomegranate concentrate, sumac, nuts and the rest of the oil, stir well and serve hot.

CREATION SPINACH

450g (1 pound) spinach
30ml (2 tablespoons) oil
4 eggs
6 scallions, chopped
4 tablespoons coriander, chopped
1 tablespoon mint, chopped
1 tablespoon tarragon, chopped
1 tablespoon dill, chopped
130g (1 cup) walnuts, chopped
Salt and pepper

1. Rinse the spinach in a colander, drain and squeeze out any excess water.
2. Place in a large pan with 30ml (2 tablespoons) of the oil and allow to wilt over a low heat, drain again.
3. In a mixing bowl, lightly beat the eggs, add the drained spinach, chopped scallions, coriander, mint, dill, walnuts, season with salt and pepper and mix well.
4. Pour the mixture into an oven dish and place in a pre-heated oven at 180C (350F) for 20 minutes. Serve hot. Can be accompanied by yogurt or green salad.

IRANIAN SPINACH

450g (1 pound) spinach
250ml (1 cup) water
1 medium onion, chopped
45g (3 tablespoons) clarified butter
1 garlic clove, crushed
250ml (1 cup) yogurt
1 teaspoon cinnamon
1 teaspoon nutmeg
Salt and pepper

1. Rinse the spinach and chop finely. Place in a pan and cover with hot water, bring to boil, lower heat and cook for 10 minutes.
2. Soften the onions in the butter.
3. Drain the spinach and squeeze out

any excess water. Add the spinach and the crushed garlic to the pan with the onions. Cook on a medium heat for about 8 minutes.

4. Remove the pan from heat, mix the yogurt, cinnamon and nutmeg through the spinach and season with salt and pepper. Can be served hot or cold.

STUFFED CHARD

900g (2 pounds) chard
200g (7 ounces) lamb, minced
200g (7 ounces) rice, rinsed
Juice of 2 lemons
or 30ml (2 tablespoons) pomegranate concentrate
2 garlic cloves, peeled
Salt and pepper

1. Cut away the stem of the chard and set aside. Wash the leaves and plunge in boiling water for about 10 seconds.
2. Lay the leaves out on a flat surface and cut them them so that they are about the size of the palm of your hand.
3. Dry fry the meat in a pan until brown and season with salt and pepper. Add the rice to the pan and stir for about 5 minutes on a medium heat.
4. Lay a small finger-sized strip of this filling onto each leaf. Roll the leaf around the stuffing using the palm of your hand.

5. Wash the stems and chop finely. Lay at the bottom of a large pan along with the garlic. Carefully arrange the stuffed chard on the bed of stems. Cover with water and the lemon juice or pomegranate concentrate.
6. Slide a lid or plate inside the pan on top of the chard rolls so they are secured into place.
7. Bring to the boil, reduce heat and simmer for 45 minutes to 1 hour depending on the thickness of the leaves; spring chard is thinner than that of the autumn. Serve hot.

CHARD WITH ONIONS

200g (7 ounces) chard
60ml (4 tablespoons) olive oil
2 onions, finely chopped
Juice of ½ a lemon
Salt

1. Wash and chop the chard. Place in a saucepan and cover with boiling water. Reduce the heat and cook for 10 minutes.
2. Drain the chard and add the onion. Cook on a medium heat for 30 minutes, stirring occasionally.
3. Drain off any excess liquid, transfer to a serving dish and serve hot.

SPICED CHARD STALKS

450g (1 pound) chard stalks
200g (7 ounces) lamb, minced
30ml (2 tablespoons) olive oil
1 teaspoon cumin
1 teaspoon dried mint
1 teaspoon saffron, crushed
Juice of 2 lemons
Salt and pepper

1. Wash and finely chop the stalks.
Place in a saucepan of boiling water
for 30 minutes. Remove and drain
in a colander.
2. Gently fry the stalks in a large pan
with the oil. Add the meat to the pan
and cook until browned.
3. Season with mint, saffron, cumin
and salt. Cover with water, bring to
the boil, reduce heat and simmer until
meat is tender and the water has
evaporated. Serve hot.

WILD LEAVES WITH MEAT

450g (1 pound) wild leaves, such as
cress, spinach, sorrel and chard.
200g (7 ounces) lamb, chopped
30ml (2 tablespoons) olive oil
2 onions, chopped
Salt

1. Wash and finely chop the leaves.
2. To blanche the leaves, place in a
saucepan of boiling water for 10
minutes. Remove, transfer to a
colander, briefly rinse with cold
water, and drain.
2. Gently soften the onions in a large
pan with the oil. Add the meat to the
pan and cook until browned.
3. Add the leaves, season and cover
with water. Simmer on a low heat
until meat is tender. Serve hot.

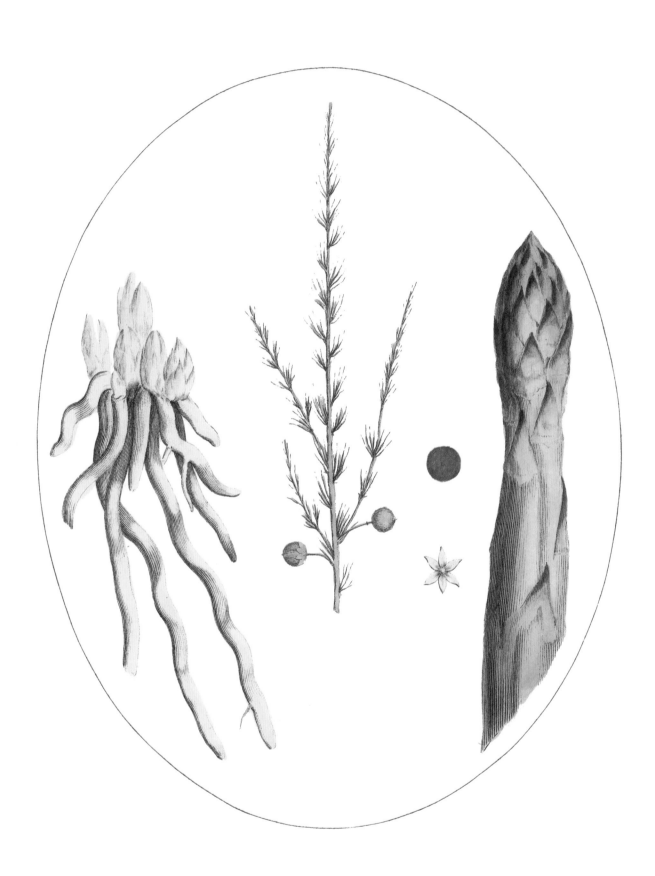

ASPARAGUS

This perennial plant is known to have been eaten in ancient Egypt and was widely appreciated by the Romans, whose sophisticated cultivation of the root is said to have been unparalleled. *Asparagus officinalis* was so popular in ancient Rome that the Emperor Augustus coined the phrase *'velocius quam asparagi coquantur'* or 'faster than you can cook asparagus'. Archaeological evidence shows that asparagus was a common feature on the ancient Levantine table. Wild asparagus even grows in the region to this day. Although certainly eaten in the Holy Land and in Egypt, asparagus goes unmentioned in the spiritual texts. As Suyuti gave it note, adding that asparagus could free blockages in the kidneys. Although there is no modern medical evidence to support this, asparagus is a nutritious vegetable, containing vitamins A and C. Although green asparagus remains the most prized in cuisine and has the highest vitamin and mineral content, purple and white varieties also exist.

ASPARAGUS WITH MEAT

450g (1 pound) asparagus
200g (7 ounces) lamb, minced
45ml (3 tablespoons) lemon juice
45g (3 tablespoons) clarified butter
or oil
Salt

1. Prepare and chop the asparagus, leaving the tips aside.

2. Gently fry the meat in a large pan with clarified butter or oil until browned. Stir in the chopped asparagus and fry for 5 minutes.
3. Season with salt and cover with water. Leave to simmer until the meat and asparagus are tender.
4. Gently steam the asparagus tips in a separate pan. Add to the mixture, squeeze with lemon juice, adjust seasonings and serve hot.

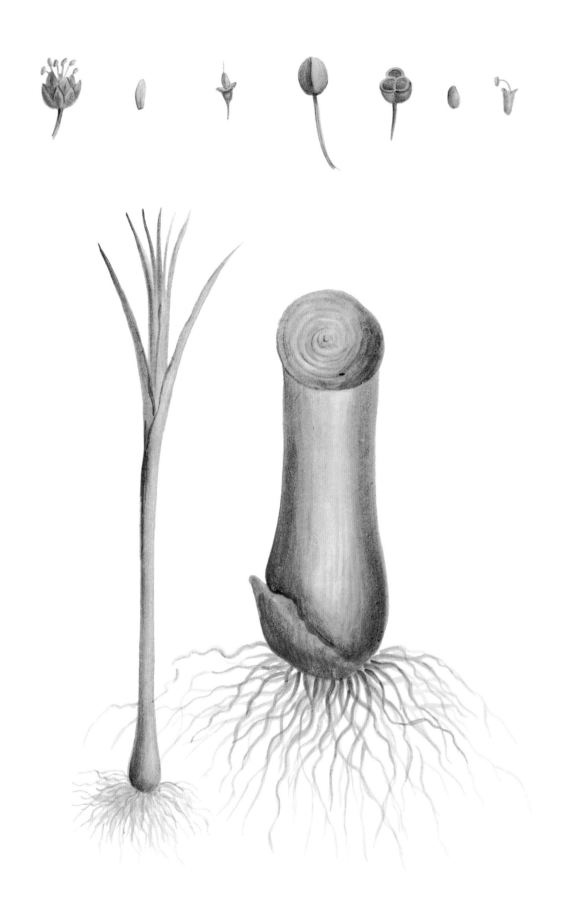

LEEKS

'We remember the fish we ate in Egypt ... the leeks, onions and the garlic ...'
NUMBERS 5:11

L eeks, or *Allium porrum*, the milder cousins of onions and garlic, were widely consumed in ancient times. The first evidence of their cultivation has been found in Egypt and is dated at around 2000 BC, but they are also known to have been consumed in ancient Sumeria. Leeks remained popular with the Hebrews after their return from Egypt and were widely eaten by the Romans. Although they have a slightly less pungent flavour than onions, they were still unpopular with Muhammad who found their odour disagreeable. Leeks are, however, very versatile in cooking. The leaves can be made into relish or, as is often the case nowadays, eaten in soups. The bulbs make a good seasoning for meat or fish, a valued ingredient in soups or they can simply be eaten alone, braised.

LEEK CASSEROLE

4 leeks, chopped
1 small head lettuce, chopped
1 cup parsley, chopped
225g (½ pound) spinach, chopped
1 spring onion, chopped
1 ½ tablespoons flour
65g (½ cup) walnuts, chopped
6 eggs
60g (4 tablespoons) clarified butter
Salt and pepper

1. Place all the chopped vegetables in a bowl and mix together. Sieve the flour into the bowl, mix well and season.

2. Beat the eggs well and add them to the vegetables and flour mixture. Mix together and then add the walnuts.
3. Melt the butter in 4 separate ovenproof dishes and spoon in the vegetable mixture.
4. Cook for 40 minutes in a pre-heated oven at 180C (350F). Serve with thick yogurt.

FISH

*'It is He who has subdued
the ocean, so that you may eat of
its fresh fish and bring up
from its depths
ornaments to wear.'*

QURAN, THE BEE 16:9

FISH

O f all the foods mentioned in the holy texts, fish hold a special importance. The Hebrews fondly remembered the fish they ate in Egypt as they
wandered hungry through the desert after the Exodus [NUMBERS 11:5].
Muhammad said that, *'the first meal of the people of paradise will be the caudal lobe of
fish liver'* [SAYING OF MUHAMMAD RELATED BY AL BUKHARI]. Fish are highly
significant in the Bible: several of the disciples themselves were fishermen and it
was broiled fish that Jesus ate after the Resurrection [LUKE 24:42]. Fish even
became the secret symbol for the early Christian Church. The Greek word for fish,
ichthus, is the sacred acrostic of Jesus Christ, Son of God, Saviour.

The consumption of fish is, however, subject to several restrictions. There is a
general taboo surrounding the eating of fish with dairy products in Islam. Indeed,
fish and dairy produce were rarely consumed together in Europe until recent times.
The fourteenth-century recipe collection *Le Viandier de Taillevent* contains eighty-
five fish recipes, in all of which dairy produce is replaced by almond milk. Even
more significant are the restrictions on eating fish imposed by Jewish Mosaic law.

*'These you may eat, of all that are in the waters. Everything in the waters that has
fins and scales, whether in the seas or in the rivers, you may eat. But anything in the
seas or the rivers that has not fins and scales, of the swarming creatures in the waters
and of the living creatures that are in the waters, is an abomination to you.'*
LEVITICUS 11:9

In brief, this meant that shellfish and crustaceans, such as crab and lobster, were
unclean and therefore forbidden, along with various other scaleless water dwellers
such as eels. The recipes in this book have been selected in accordance with these
rules and traditions.

Fish was often perceived as poor man's food that was less nutritious than meat.
Fridays were ruled as meatless by the Vatican, and thus for centuries fish was com-

monly perceived as the fare of abstinence. Today, the nutritional value of fish has been rediscovered. Low in saturated fat and low in calories, it is perceived to be a healthier dietary protein source than meat. It is also an excellent source of omega-3 essential fatty acids, which help reduce the chances of coronary heart disease. Fish has anti-inflammatory qualities and perhaps can even help in the fight against cancer.

Meat was generally preferred in the Holy Land, but fish was everyday fare along the coast and in areas with rivers and lakes, such as Galilee. Over forty species of freshwater fish are found in the Sea of Galilee and its surrounding area. They often swam in large schools, making for substantial catches by the Galilean fishermen. However, there are no references to any particular types of fish in the Holy texts. In the story of Jonah, some modern translations have alluded to a 'whale', whereas others only mention 'a large fish' [JONAH 1:17]. In the thirteenth-century recipe book *Kitab al Tabikh*, the author writes that freshwater fish are better than those from the sea. The opinion of the author was probably determined by the proximity of the Tigris and the Euphrates. Holy Land fish, such as the sardines of the Sea of Galilee, were commonly dried. Many of these were often exported to Rome where they were used to produce *garum*, a condiment similar to modern day Vietnamese *nuoc nam*.

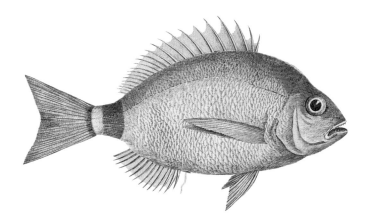

ST. PETER'S FISH

'They gave him a piece of broiled fish and he took it and ate it in their presence.'
LUKE 24:42

The fish Jesus ate in front of his frightened apostles following the resurrection was most likely to have been a local one such as St. Peter's fish, which is widely believed to be Tilapia *(Tilapia galilea)*. The apostles probably simply marinaded and grilled it over an open fire.

900g (2 pounds) tilapia fish
2 garlic cloves, crushed
2 teaspoons cumin
Juice of 1 lemon
15ml (1 tablespoon) olive oil
Salt and pepper

1. Clean and prepare the fish.
2. Mix the garlic, cumin and salt together. Stir in the lemon juice and then the oil.
3. Smear the marinade over the fish and leave to marinate in a cool place for 1 hour.
4. Pre-heat the grill and cook the fish for about 5 minutes on each side, depending on their size. Alternatively the fish can be placed on a hot barbecue.

GALILEE GRILLED SARDINES

'When they had gone ashore they saw a charcoal fire there, with fish on it and bread. Jesus said, "bring some of the fish that you have just caught."'
JOHN 21:9–10

Galilee sardines *(Acanthobrama terraesanctae)* were common at the time of Jesus. The book of John describes how Jesus and the disciples, many of whom were fishermen, prepared a simple breakfast of fish and bread on the shores of Galilee. Grilled sardines, from anywhere in the world, make a hearty breakfast or a light meal.

900g (2 pounds) sardines,
1 lemon, thinly sliced
Salt and pepper
4 flat bread loaves, to serve

1. Rub the scales off the sardines under cold running water, cut off the fins and make an incision along the belly of the fish to remove the guts. Wash out the cavity of the fish with a little cold water. A good fishmonger should prepare the sardines on demand.
2. Generously rub each fish, including the cavities, with sea salt. Place the lemon slices in the cavities and leave to stand for 30 minutes.

3. Rub away any excess salt and remove the lemon. Place the fish under a pre-heated very hot grill or on a hot barbecue for about 3–5 minutes on each side. Alternatively skewer each fish with a wooden stick and grill over an open wood fire. Serve hot or cold with flat bread and a green salad if desired.

ABRAHAM'S FISH

Red mullet is known as the king of fish in the Arab world, and is often called *Sultan Ibrahim* after the patriarch Abraham.

4 red mullet, de-scaled and gutted
2 lemons, thinly sliced
½ teaspoon cumin
45ml (3 tablespoons) olive oil
Salt and pepper

1. Combine the salt, pepper and cumin and rub on the outside of the fish. Place the lemon slices in the cavities.
2. Leave to stand at room temperature for 1 hour. Discard the lemons.
3. Sieve some flour onto a plate and dust the fish by rolling in the flour.
4. Coat the inside of a covered earthenware casserole with olive oil. Place the fish in the casserole and cook for 15–20 minutes, depending on its thickness, at 250C (500F). Serve hot.

LAODICEA TURBOT

'Give my greeting to the brothers and sisters in Laodicea, and to Nympha and the church in her house.' COLOSSIANS 4:15

Named by Antiochus II after his wife, the banking and trading centre of *Laodicea ad lyceum* stood at the mouth of the river Lycus. It was so prosperous that when it was destroyed by an earthquake in 60 AD, it was rebuilt without any aid from Rome. The wealthy citizens of Laodicea, many of whom were part of the early Christian church, would have enjoyed luxuries such as saffron-covered fish.

4 turbot fillets
Salt
3 lemons, sliced
2 teaspoons saffron

1. Prepare the fish, rub with salt and leave to stand for 20 minutes. Rub away any excess salt.
2. Place a layer of lemons in a non-metal baking dish. Lay the fish on top and cover with the rest of the lemon.
3. Dissolve the saffron in enough water to cover the fish and lemon. Cover and leave in the liquid overnight.
4. Remove the fish and pat dry. Place under a hot grill or on a barbecue and cook on both sides until tender. Serve hot with rice.

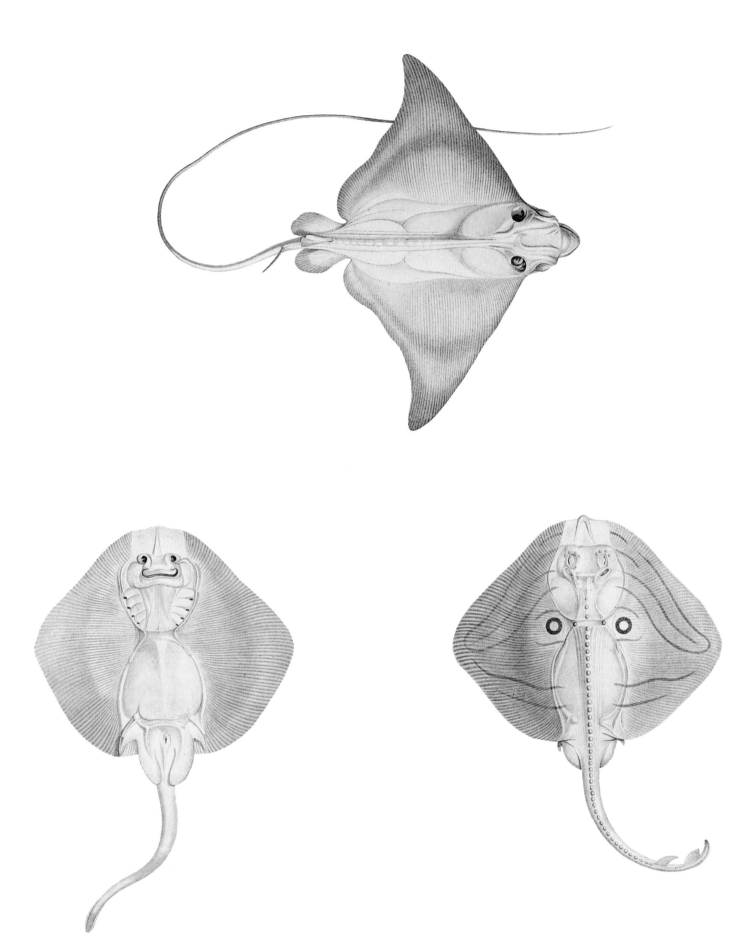

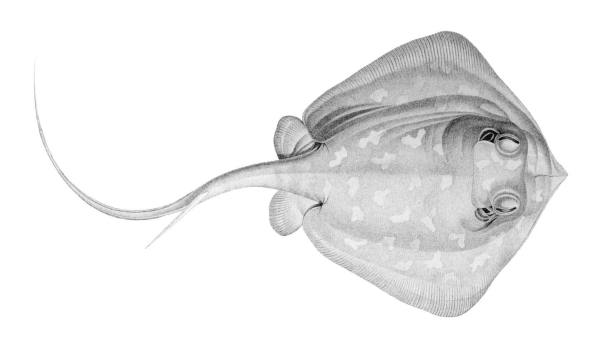

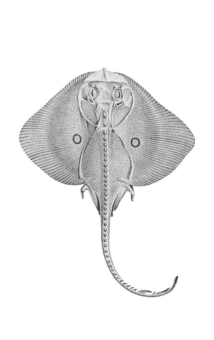

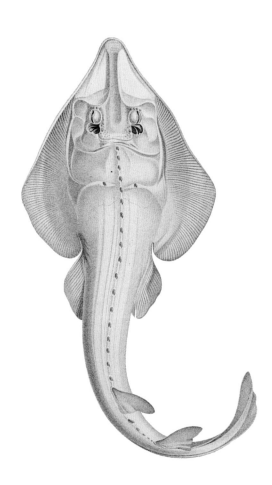

TARSUS SKEWERED SWORDFISH

St. Paul, or Saul as he was known in the Holy Land, was born in the town of Tarsus, capital of Cilicia. He returned there after the crucifixion until Barnabas sought his help to spread the gospel in Antioch. Skewered swordfish remains popular in the region, part of modern Turkey.

900g (2 pounds) swordfish
Marinade:
Juice of ½ a lemon
30ml (2 tablespoons) olive oil
1 small onion, sliced
2 bay leaves, crumbled
Salt and pepper
Dipping sauce:
60ml (4 tablespoons) olive oil
Juice of ½ lemon
½ cup parsley, chopped
Salt and pepper

1. Skin the fish and cut into cubes.
2. Whisk the marinade ingredients together in a large bowl, add the fish and leave in a cool place for 4 hours. Move fish occasionally to spread the marinade evenly.
3. Thread the fish onto 4 skewers and cook over glowing charcoal, or on a griddle pan, for 20 minutes. The inside of the fish will cook better on metal skewers. Turn the fish at regular intervals, brushing with the marinade.

4. Combine the lemon juice, oil, salt, pepper and parsley together to make the dipping sauce. Serve the fish hot accompanied by the dipping sauce.

KHALID'S FISH WITH DATES

This recipe reflects the Arabian influence in the Holy land following the Islamic conquests, which were completed under the caliph Khalid bin al Walid.

160g (1 cup) whole dried dates, pitted
4 firm-fleshed fish, such as red mullet
1 small onion, finely chopped
2 teaspoons Antioch spice mix
¼ teaspoon saffron
Salt
For the Arabian spice mix:
1 teaspoon black peppercorns, ground
½ teaspoon coriander seeds, ground
½ teaspoon cloves, ground
¾ teaspoon cumin seeds, ground
½ teaspoon whole nutmeg, ground

1. Soak the dried dates in cold water for 30 minutes.
2. Clean and gut the fish, remove the scales by running cold water over the fish and scraping off the scales. Sprinkle with salt and leave to stand for 20 minutes.
3. Mix the onion with the spice mix and add a little water until it forms a

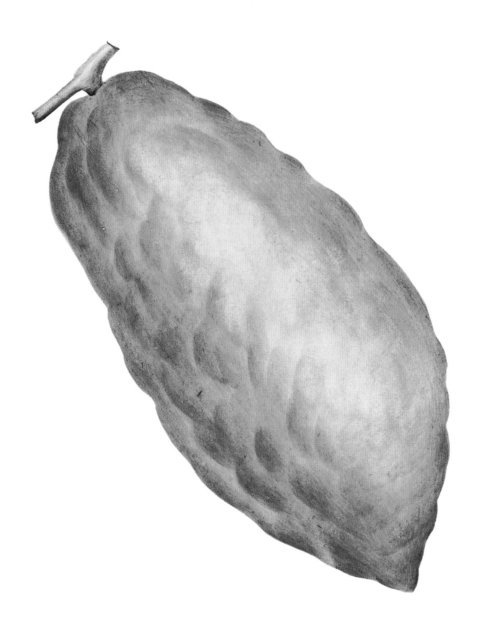

paste. Stuff paste into the cavities of the fish and seal with cocktail sticks.

4. Puree the dates so that they form a soft paste, add water if necessary. Spread the paste on each side of the fish and leave to stand on a rack or wire tray for 20 minutes.

5. Cook over a hot barbecue or under a pre-heated grill for 5 to 10 minutes each side, depending on the size of the fish. Serve hot.

SPICED MACKEREL

Mackerel was not the fish of choice in the ancient world, but grilled simply with lemon and herbs it makes for a pleasant dish. The dill in this recipe gives the mackerel an extra bite. A dish such as this one would have been enjoyed by a fisherman and his family after he had sold his more valuable produce for the day.

4 mackerel, gutted and butterflied
1 lemon, sliced
15ml (1 tablespoon) olive oil
45ml (3 tablespoons) lemon juice
1 teaspoon coriander seeds
1 teaspoon dill
½ teaspoon black peppercorns, ground
2 tablespoons parsley, finely chopped

1. To butterfly the fish run a sharp knife down the backbone. Gently remove the spine and as little flesh as possible. Open out the fish and remove any guts and excess bones. Wash the fish under cold water and pat dry. Lay the lemon slices on the flesh side, fold back together and leave to stand for 20 minutes.

2. Heat 1 tablespoon of oil in a pan with some ground coriander seeds, peppercorns, dill and crushed garlic, cook until the aromas are released, without letting the garlic colour. Pour the mixture over the fish.

3. Place the fish on a lightly oiled baking tray and cook in a pre-heated oven at 200C (400F) for about 10 minutes or more if thick.

4. Squeeze 3 tablespoons of lemon juice into the pan, stir and pour immediately over the mackerel. Garnish with chopped parsley and serve hot or cold.

ON FRYING FISH

In the early Islamic period it was widely believed that fish was most wholesome when fried. This stemmed from a belief that the wet humours of the fish were unhealthy and needed to be balanced out. Cooks would go to great lengths to dry out fish by salting prior to cooking. Frying fish remains the most popular way to cook fish in the Levant to this day. Fish were salted, dipped in flour, sometimes mixed with cumin and fried until tender. They were served with lemon when it was available. As oil was an expensive commodity, deep frying was a cooking method of the wealthy. It is important to remember that the temperature of the oil varies for large and small fish when deep frying. When cooking larger fish the oil should be moderately hot to prevent the outside of the fish from burning before the inside is cooked. Fish were generally cooked in olive oil or in sesame oil when the former was unavailable.

SIDONIAN FRIED FISH WITH ROSEMARY

An important fishing port, Sidon was visited by Jesus on his northernmost journey. St. Paul also stopped there on his way to Rome. Several fish are suitable for this simple yet delicious recipe, such as sea bass, sea bream, lemon sole or skate.

4 fish
Plain flour, sieved
Mild olive oil, for frying
2 garlic cloves, chopped
1 teaspoon rosemary spines
60ml (4 tablespoons) vinegar
Salt and pepper

1. Prepare the fish, rub with salt and leave to stand for 15 minutes.
2. Sieve some flour onto a plate and roll the fish so that it is dusted.
3. Fill a pan with oil 3cm (1 inch) in depth. Heat thoroughly and fry the fish on each side until golden, drain and set aside.
4. Discard all but 60ml (4 tablespoons) of the oil. Add the garlic, rosemary and fry. Sprinkle 1 tablespoon of flour into the pan and stir over a medium heat until lightly coloured.
5. Remove pan from the heat and pour in the vinegar, ensuring that it does not spit. Return to heat and cook for about 2 minutes, season and serve hot poured over the fish.

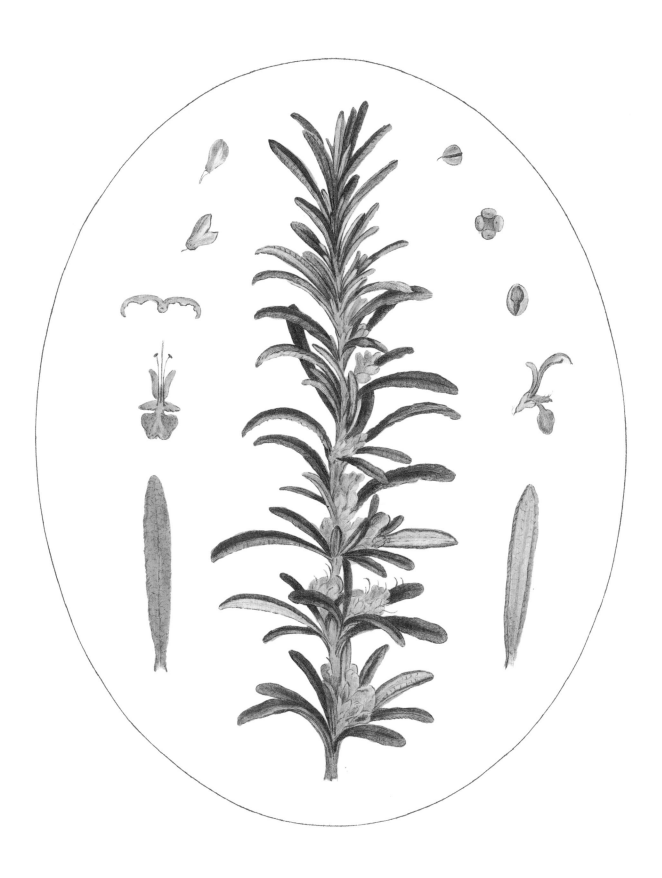

ABBASID FRIED FISH PARCELS

This recipe is influenced by the thirteenth-century Baghdad cookery book *Kitab al Tabikh*, which was based on a collection of earlier recipes. Although this recipe was most likely prepared with the small Mesopotamian river fish, *tirikh*, a number of fish are suitable for it, such as red mullet, trout, sea bream, hake or skate.

900g (2 pounds) fish fillets with skin.
1 garlic clove, crushed
1 teaspoon thyme
½ teaspoon cumin
½ teaspoon coriander
½ teaspoon cinnamon
½ teaspoon saffron
60ml (4 tablespoons) sesame oil

1. Cut the fillets in pieces that can be easily folded over.
2. Grind the thyme, cumin, coriander and cinnamon together using a pestle and mortar. Mix in the crushed garlic and 15ml (1 tablespoon) of sesame oil to form a paste. Spoon the paste inside and outside the fillet pieces, fold over and secure with cocktail sticks.
3. Heat the remaining oil in a pan and stir in the saffron. Fry the fish on either side for about 5 to 10 minutes. The fish should take on the yellow colour of the saffron. Serve hot.

BABYLONIAN FRIED FISH

900g (2 pounds) white fish
1 teaspoon coriander
30ml (2 tablespoons) sesame oil
60ml (4 tablespoons) white vinegar
1 teaspoon saffron

1. Clean and prepare the fish. Remove the skin and cut into bite-sized pieces.
2. Dissolve the saffron in the vinegar and stir well.
3. Heat the sesame oil in a pan. Stir in the coriander and fry the pieces of fish for about 5 minutes on both sides, depending on their thickness.
4. Pour the saffron and vinegar mix over the fish and cook for 2 minutes. Turn the fish so that they are completely coloured with the yellow liquid. Serve hot with rice.

ZEBEDEE'S TROUT

'Follow me and I will make you fish for people.' MATTHEW 4:19

Zebedee was a successful fisherman on the Sea of Galilee. When Jesus challenged his sons James and John to follow him and spread the gospel, Zebedee was left to manage the family business on his own without the help of his apostle sons.

900g (2 pounds) trout fillets
60g (½ cup) walnuts, finely chopped
1 spring onion, finely chopped
1 tablespoon dill, finely chopped
30ml (2 tablespoons) vinegar
60ml (4 tablespoons) walnut oil
30ml (2 tablespoons) olive oil
200g (7 ounces) mixed leaves, such as
rocket and cress
Salt and pepper

1. Whisk the vinegar and a little salt
together until it begins to froth.
Slowly pour in the walnut oil and
1 tablespoon of olive oil and season.
Mix in the dill and finely chopped
spring onion.
2. Lay the trout fillets on a lightly-
oiled grilling pan skin side down. Grill
for about 10 minutes or to taste.
3. Fry the walnuts with the remainder
of the olive oil without letting
them burn.
4. Toss the washed and dried mixed
leaves in half of the dressing. Serve the
fish fillets on a bed of leaves, drizzled
with the remainder of the dressing and
garnished with the chopped walnuts.

FISH AND OLIVE STEW

Slow-cooked fish in earthenware
vessels was popular in ancient times.
The receptacle was buried in the
embers of a fire or in hot sands. The
spread of Islam through North Africa
brought about the merger of Arab and
Berber culinary traditions. The result
is dishes such as the Maghreb tajine,
which is akin to this ancient method of
cooking. Firm-fleshed fish, such as red
mullet, monkfish, cod and haddock,
are best suited to these recipes.

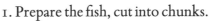

900g (2 pounds) fish
4 tablespoons coriander, chopped
2 garlic cloves, crushed
Juice of 2 lemons
1 teaspoon cumin
250ml (1 cup) olive oil
450g (1 pound) carrots
20 black olives, pitted
10 black olives, whole
Salt

1. Prepare the fish, cut into chunks.
2. Combine the coriander, cumin,
crushed garlic, salt, lemon juice and oil
in a mixing bowl. Place the fish in the
bowl and leave to marinate for 3 hours
in a cool place.
3. Cut the carrots into batons and
steam in a moistened tajine or earthenware vessel on a medium heat for
20 minutes.
4. Add the marinated fish, pitted
olives, 125ml (½ cup) of water and
125ml (½ cup) of the marinade. Mix
well. Garnish with the whole olives.
5. Cook over a medium stove for 40
minutes and serve hot.

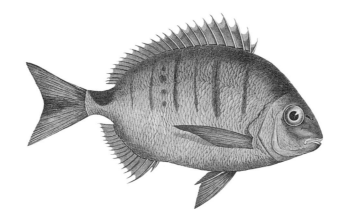

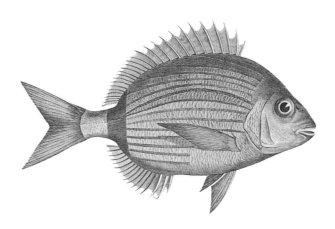

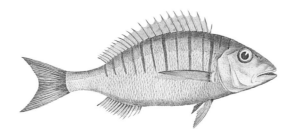

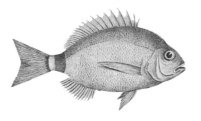

TAJINE ABDUL RAHMAN

Abdul Rahman was the only surviving member of his clan, who were murdered at a luncheon massacre at their Damascus palace. As the slayers set up a new caliphate in Baghdad, Abdul left the Near East and travelled west across North Africa to Spain where he set up a rival caliphate. Dishes such as this one emerged as he passed through the Maghreb, leaving touches of Damascus on Berber culture and cuisine.

900g (2 pounds) firm-fleshed fish
4 tablespoons coriander, chopped
2 garlic cloves
Juice of 2 lemons
1 teaspoon cumin
125ml (½ cup) olive oil
1 preserved lemon, sliced
1 onion, sliced into rings
Salt

1. Prepare the fish and cut into chunks.
2. Combine the coriander, crushed garlic, cumin, salt, lemon juice, and oil together in a mixing bowl. Place the fish in the bowl and leave to marinate for 3 hours in a cool place.
3. Lay a bed of onion rings at the bottom of the cooking vessel. Place the fish on the bed, and cover with 250ml (1 cup) of the marinade and 250ml (1 cup) of water.

4. Cook over a medium stove for 40 minutes. Serve garnished with slices of preserved lemon.

SWEET APOLLONIAN FISH

The Levantine coastal town of Apollonia was one of the many Mediterranean settlements named after the Greek god Apollo. This sweet, succulent dish reflects the Greek influence in the Levant and would have surely been deemed fit for a god. It is best prepared with a tender fish such as sea bass.

4 whole sea bass
60ml (4 tablespoons) olive oil
Juice of 2 lemons
1 lemon, cut into wedges
450g (1 pound) onions
60ml (4 tablespoons) honey
Salt and pepper

1. Clean and prepare the fish. Rub with salt and lemon then leave to stand for 20 minutes.
2. Gently fry the onions with a little of the oil until soft. Stir in the honey and half of the lemon juice, season and cook for another 5 minutes.
3. Mix the oil and the rest of the lemon juice together and season with salt and pepper. Brush onto the fish and place in a baking dish.

4. Cook in a pre-heated oven at 180C for 15 minutes.
5. Serve the fish on a bed of onions, garnished with lemon wedges.

OVEN BAKED JOHN DORY

2 medium-sized John Dory
60ml (4 tablespoons) olive oil
Salt
½ teaspoon dried coriander
1 lemon, thinly sliced
Juice of 1 lemon
2 garlic cloves, thinly sliced

1. Clean and prepare the fish including the cavity. Mix the salt and coriander together and rub inside and outside the fish.
2. Place the lemon and garlic slices in the cavity and some on top of the fish. Leave to marinate in a cool place for 2 hours.
3. Remove the lemon and garlic and drain the fish of any liquid. Transfer to an olive oil-coated oven dish.
4. Bake in a pre-heated oven at 160C (320F). Squeeze the juice of the remaining lemon over the fish to break up any excess oil.
Serve hot.

ROCK SALT FISH

Salt, the king of seasonings, was taken from the mines of the Dead Sea, the principal source in the Holy Land. Fish encased in salt would have been placed in an earthenware vessel, then put directly in an open fire or oven.

4 sea bream,
4 tablespoons parsley, chopped
1 lemon, thinly sliced
3kg (about 7 pounds) rock salt

1. Prepare the fish. Remove the scales by running it under a cold tap and rubbing the scales.
2. Place the parsley and lemon slices in the cleaned cavities of the fish.
3. Cover a large roasting pan or fill a suitably sized earthenware cooking vessel with a thick layer of rock salt and lay the fish on top. Cover the fish with the remainder of the salt and press down on the salt adding water in order to create a compact crust around the fish.
4. Place in a pre-heated oven at 250C (500F) and cook for 15 to 20 minutes.
5. Crack into the crust and remove all the salt from the fish before serving hot.

TYRE BAKED TAHINA FISH

Tyre was one of the most important Phoenician port towns. Situated on an offshore island, it was a cosmopolitan port and a centre of Mediterranean trade. Sesame or *tahina* sauce has been and remains a favourite in the region and indeed all over the Levant throughout the ages. This recipe is suitable for any white fish, such as sea bass, turbot, monkfish or cod. It can be served either hot or cold.

4 fish fillets
Salt
2 onions, thinly sliced
45ml (3 tablespoons) extra-virgin olive oil
190ml (¾ cup) sesame seed paste
Juice of 2 lemons
250ml (1 cup) water
½ cup flat-leaved parsley, chopped
2 lemons, cut into wedges
4 tablespoons pomegranate seeds

1. Rub the fish with salt and set aside for 20 minutes.
2. Gently fry the onions with 1 tablespoon of the oil in a covered pan until soft.
3. Whisk the sesame seed paste with the lemon juice and some water until they form a white creamy sauce and season with salt.
3. Place the onions in a non-metal baking dish and lay the fish on top. Bake in a pre-heated oven at 200C (400F) for 20 minutes.
4. Remove the dish from the oven and cover the fish with the sauce. Lower the oven to 160C (320F) and cook for another 5–10 minutes. Serve garnished with parsley, pomegranate seeds and lemon wedges.

CAPERS

'The prophet, may Allah bless him and grant him peace, came out to us and said, "The fire laughed and out came truffles, and the earth laughed – and out came capers."' SAYING OF MUHAMMAD RELATED BY IBN ABBAS, IN AS SUYUTI

Capers or caper berries are the unopened flower buds of the plant *Capparis spinosa*. This plant grew wild in the Levant but has been cultivated now for thousands of years. As Suyuti wrote that they were good for the spleen, but mainly they are employed for their taste. It is possible to find the fruit of the plant called caper berries in Mediterranean countries, but small capers preserved in brine or salt are more commonly found. All types make a good accompaniment to fish.

FISH WITH CAPERS

900g (2 pounds) white fish
4 tablespoons capers
15g (1 tablespoon) clarified butter
Juice of ½ a lemon
1 garlic clove
15ml (1 tablespoon) vinegar
Salt and pepper

1. Prepare the fish and rub with salt. Place in an oven dish with a tight lid.
2. Heat the butter in the pan, add the capers and garlic and fry for several minutes. Add the vinegar and lemon juice and season with salt and pepper.
3. Cover the fish with the sauce. Cook in a pre-heated oven at 180C (350F) for 10–15 minutes. Serve hot.

SKATE IN BROWNED CAPER BUTTER

900g (2 pounds) skate
200g (7 ounces) clarified butter
4 tablespoons capers
Juice of 2 lemons
Salt and pepper

1. Wash the prepared fish in cold water. Pour 1 litre of hot water into a large pan with 200ml of vinegar and a little salt. Bring to the boil and carefully add the fish to the pan. Poach the fish for 10 minutes.
2. Gently heat the butter in a frying pan until it becomes a nutty-brown colour. Add the capers and lemons and cook for 1–2 minutes. Season.
3. Skin the fish and lay on a serving platter. Pour the sauce over the fish. Serve hot.

FISH STOCK

1 fish head and bones
1 litre (4 cups) water
Parsley, lemon
1 bay leaf
Black peppercorns
Handful of sorrel
Salt and pepper

1. Place the fish in a saucepan and cover with water. Bring to the boil and skim off any residue that forms.
2. Add the lemon, parsley, bay leaf, sorrel and season with salt and pepper. Cover and simmer for 45 minutes. Leave to cool and strain before using.

RICE WITH FISH

Fish stock, *see above*
450g (1 pound) white fish, such as cod, prepared and cut into pieces
30ml (2 tablespoons) olive oil
3 onions, finely chopped
1 teaspoon cinnamon
1 bay leaf
200g (1 cup) long-grain rice
30g (¼ cup) pine nuts
2 tablespoons parsley, chopped
Salt and pepper

1. Gently fry the onions with the oil until soft. Stir in the cinnamon, salt and pepper. Gently place the fish pieces and the bay leaf in the pan and cover with the heated fish stock.
2. Bring to the boil and reduce heat. Cover and leave to simmer for 5 minutes. Remove the fish and set aside in a warm place.
3. Add the rice to the pan. Bring to boil again and reduce heat. Place a cloth in between the pan and a tightly fitting lid so as to absorb the excess moisture. Leave to simmer on a very low heat for 15–20 minutes.
4. Fry the pine nuts in a little oil without letting them blacken. Spoon the rice out on a serving dish and place the fish on top. Garnish with pine nuts and the chopped parsley.

MOSES SOLE

Legend has it that this delicate thin fish was split into two when Moses parted the Red Sea. Consequently it is often known as *Samak Mousa* or Moses sole. Sole can be simply grilled, poached or baked, but this Roman recipe is an interesting way to prepare the fish.

4 sole
2 eggs, beaten
500ml (2 cups) chicken stock
30ml (2 tablespoons) vinegar
2 leeks, finely chopped
½ teaspoon coriander
½ teaspoon oregano
15ml (1 tablespoon) oil
Salt

1. Prepare and skin the sole.
2. Place the leeks in a large pan with the heated oil. Stir in the oregano, season with salt and cook for 5 minutes. Cover with 450ml (1 pint) of chicken stock, add vinegar, cover and cook on a medium heat for 20 minutes.
3. Gently lay the sole in the pan and cook for 5 minutes or more to taste. Remove the fish and set aside on a hot serving platter.
4. Mix the beaten eggs into the sauce and cook for about 2 minutes. Pour the sauce over the fish and serve hot sprinkled with black pepper.

FISH IN PARADISE SAUCE

Luxurious sauces such as this one are traditionally served at feasts in the Middle East. This sauce is best suited to delicately steamed sole, sea bass or John Dory.

4 fish fillets
125ml (½ cup) pomegranate concentrate
125ml (½ cup) olive oil
65g (½ cup) walnuts, finely chopped
½ cup dried pieces of bread
250ml (1 cup) water
1 teaspoon cumin
1 teaspoon ginger, grated
1 spring onion, finely chopped (optional)
Salt

1. Whisk the pomegranate concentrate, water and oil together. Mix in the walnuts, dried pieces of bread and onion. Stir in the cumin and ginger, season with salt.
2. Bake the fish fillets in a pre-heated oven at 180C (350F) for 15–20 minutes. Cover with sauce and serve hot or cold.

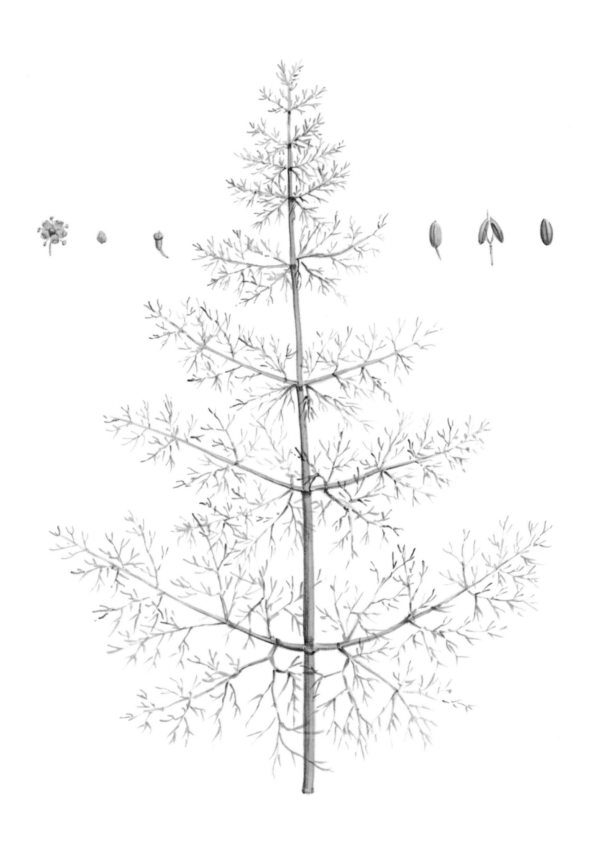

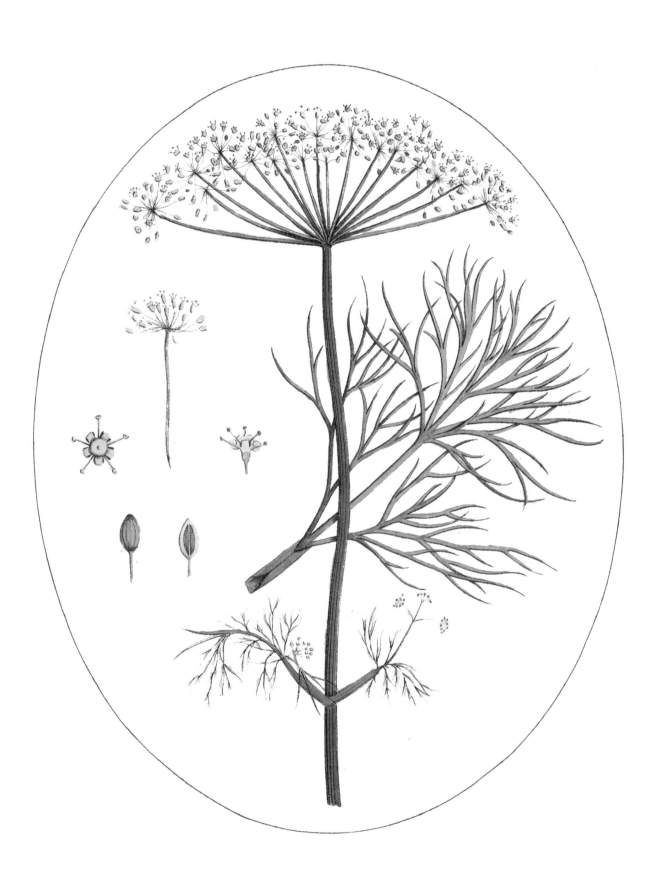

DILL

'Dill is not threshed with a threshing sledge, nor is a cart wheel rolled over cummin; but dill is beaten out with a stick, and cummin with a rod.' ISAIAH 28:27

In some versions of the Bible this umbellifer is referred to as 'anise', although scholars generally agree that this refers to dill. A common garden plant, dill resembles parsley or fennel in its appearance. *Anethum graveolens* contains aromatic seeds, similar to caraway, that are often used in pickles. The seeds can also be distilled to produce dill-water, which contains oil commonly used in medicine. Dill is native to Southern Europe and Western Asia and is traditionally used as an accompaniment to fish in cuisine. It is said to be a good diurectic, and has certain carminative properties. A natural sedative, dill-water can be used to calm teething babies and indeed the word in English comes from the Norse verb *dilla,* which means 'to soothe'.

ROMAN DILLED MULLET

4 red mullet
60ml (4 tablespoons) oil
250ml (1 cup) chicken stock
4 leeks
2 tablespoons dill, chopped
30ml (2 tablespoons) vinegar
30ml (2 tablespoons) grape syrup
1 tablespoon flour, sieved
2 tablespoons coriander, chopped
Salt and pepper

1. Prepare the fish and de-scale it by running it under a cold tap and rubbing off the scales.
2. Mix the vinegar, half of the oil and grape syrup in a small bowl.
3. Heat some oil in a large pan. Fry the fish on each side for about 2 minutes, depending on thickness, and set aside.
4. Place the finely chopped leeks in the pan and stir until they are coated in oil. Lay the fish on the leeks, cover with chicken stock and stir in the dill. Cook on a medium heat for about 10 minutes.
5. Heat the oil and grape syrup mix in a small pan. Bind the flour into the mixture and pour over the fish. Serve hot garnished with coriander and black pepper.

POULTRY

*'We caused the clouds to
draw their shadow over you
and sent down for you manna
and quails, saying, "Eat of
the good things we have
given you."'*
QURAN, THE COW 2:55–61.

POULTRY

The book of Genesis recounts the appearance of birds at the creation of the world. *'Let the birds fly over the earth and across the dome of the sky'* [GENESIS 1:20]. In Deuteronomy the Hebrews are told, *'You may eat any winged creatures'* [DEUTERONOMY 14:20]. Restrictions on eating fowl were outlined later in the Pentateuch: *'These you shall regard as detestable among the birds. They shall not be eaten; they are an abomination. The eagle, the vulture, the osprey, the buzzard, the kite of any kind; every raven of any kind, the ostrich, the nighthawk, the sea gull, the hawk of any kind, the little owl, the cormorant, the great owl, the water hen, the desert owl, the carrion vulture, the stork, the heron of any kind, the hoopoe, and the bat'* [LEVITICUS 11:13]. Fowl were popular food in the Holy Land and more accessible to the people than meat. Birds enjoyed in the ancient Levant included quail, partridge, duck, pigeon or squab, partridge and goose. Chicken could be found in the ancient Holy Land but only became important in dietary terms during the Byzantine Empire. Today, the popularity of chicken has meant that all but the specialist butcher (and the French) have forgotten other, once popular fowl. Poultry is a good source of protein and is now eaten more and more as an alternative to red meat. Turkey has not been included in these recipes, as it was not introduced to the Levant from the Americas until the sixteenth century.

DUCK

Duck was widely enjoyed in the ancient world. It was hunted wild on the banks of the Nile as well as raised in ancient Egypt, where the meat was often preserved in salt. Duck is described in Aristotle's history of animals simply as one of the larger species of web-footed birds. Despite our knowing that duck was enjoyed throughout the ancient world, there is very little mention of the bird in holy texts. Their omission from the Bible could perhaps be due to the use of the word partridge to refer to several birds. As Suyuti says only that duck is 'hotter' than chicken.

HONEYED DUCK

1.8k g (4 pound) duck
30ml (2 tablespoons) oil
125ml (½ cup) honey
Salt and pepper

1. Rub the cleaned and prepared duck with oil and pepper. Pierce the bird in several places so that the fat is released during the cooking process. Place in a cold oven and set to 220C (450F) and cook for 30 minutes.
2. Reduce the heat to 200C (400F). Season with salt and cook for another hour or more to taste.
3. Remove the duck and smear with honey. Return to the oven and cook for 30 minutes, ensuring that the honey does not burn. Serve hot.

DUCK WITH OLIVES

1 duck
200g (7 ounces) green olives
3 garlic cloves
750ml (3 cups) chicken stock
1 onion, finely chopped
1 shallot, finely chopped
2 bay leaves
1 tablespoon flour, sieved
30g (2 tablespoons) clarified butter
15ml (1 tablespoon) olive oil
Salt and pepper

1. Rub the cleaned and prepared duck with oil and pepper. Pierce the bird in several places so that the fat is released during the cooking process.
2. Rub the cleaned cavity with salt and garlic and stuff with half of the olives and the remaining garlic, chopped. Season with salt and pepper.
3. Heat the oil and butter in a large

heavy-based pan, brown the duck on all sides. Remove after 30 minutes.

4. Add the onion and shallot to the pan and fry until golden.

5. Pour the stock into the pan and slowly whisk in the flour. Add the bay leaves to the pan and reduce the sauce on a low heat for 20 minutes.

6. Add the remaining olives to the sauce and return the duck to the pan. Cover and cook for a further 20 minutes on a medium heat. Serve the hot duck on a platter surrounded by the remaining olives.

DUCK WITH PEACHES

1.8kg (4 pounds) duck
30ml (2 tablespoons) olive oil
450g (1 pound) firm peaches
Salt and pepper

1. Rub the cleaned and prepared duck with oil and pepper. Pierce the bird in several places so that the fat is released during the cooking process. Place in an oven and set the temperature at 220C (450F) and cook for 30 minutes.

2. Reduce the heat to 200C (400F), baste and season with salt and cook for another hour or more to taste.

3. Peel and stone the peaches, then poach the peaches for 10 minutes in boiling water. Place in a pan and leave to simmer for 30 minutes.

4. Remove the duck from the oven and spoon off any excess fat from the pan. Cover the bird with the peaches. Return to the oven and cook for 30 minutes. Serve the hot duck on a platter surrounded by the peaches.

POMEGRANATE ROAST DUCK

1.8kg (4 pounds) duck
30g (2 tablespoons) clarified butter
1 large onion, finely chopped
130g (1 cup) walnuts, finely chopped
65g (½ cup) walnuts, coarsely ground
250ml (1 cup) pomegranate concentrate
45g (3 tablespoons) sugar
2 cinnamon sticks
15ml (1 tablespoon) lemon juice
2 tablespoons pomegranate seeds
Salt and pepper

1. Rub the cleaned and prepared duck with oil and pepper. Pierce the bird in several places so that the fat is released during the cooking process.

2. Brown the duck on all sides in a large pan with half of the butter.

3. Transfer the duck to a cold oven, set the temperature at 220C (450F) and cook for 30 minutes. Baste the bird and reduce the temperature to 200C (400F) and cook for 1 hour and 30 minutes or more according to taste, basting occasionally with the sauce.

4. While the duck is cooking, place the remaining butter in a frying pan and gently fry the onion until transparent. Add all walnuts, pomegranate concentrate, sugar and cinnamon to a seperate pan. Bring mixture to the boil, reduce heat and leave to simmer. Pour a small quantity of the sauce over duck and baste every 20 minutes. Add lemon juice during this time, then season.

5. Transfer duck to a heated serving dish. Spoon the remaining sauce over duck and serve covered with chopped walnuts and pomegranate seeds. Decorate with cinnamon sticks and serve with rice.

POMEGRANATE

'It is He who brings gardens into being : creepers and upright trees, the palm and all manner of crops, olives, and pomegranates alike and different. Eat of these fruits when they ripen and give away what is due of them upon the harvest day.'
QURAN, CATTLE 6:141

Of all the fruits of the ancient Levant, the pomegranate, with its bright green leaves and symmetrical rose-red fruit, is certainly one of the most beautiful. *Punica granatum* is thought to have originated in Persia and is said to have been grown in ancient Egypt and in the Hanging Gardens of Babylon. In Greek mythology, Peresphone swallowed six pomegranate seeds, sealing her fate in the underworld and prompting her mother Demeter to create winter on earth. Seeds have been found at Bronze Age sites in the Holy Land and frequent reference is made to the fruit throughout the Bible. A pomegranate was brought back by the Hebrew scouts to show Moses and his people that the fruit existed in the Holy Land [NUMBERS 13:23]. Although it was appreciated for its medicinal properties, the pomegranate was most valued for the bitter but intensely refreshing red juice of its many seeds. The number of seeds saw Hebrews interpret the fruit as a symbol of fertility. Muhammad was also fond of pomegranates, and said that each fruit contained at least one pip from the Garden of Eden. He is reported to have said, *'Whoever eats pomegranates has the light of Allah in his heart!'* [SAYING OF MUHAMMAD RELATED BY ʿALI, IN AS SUYUTI].

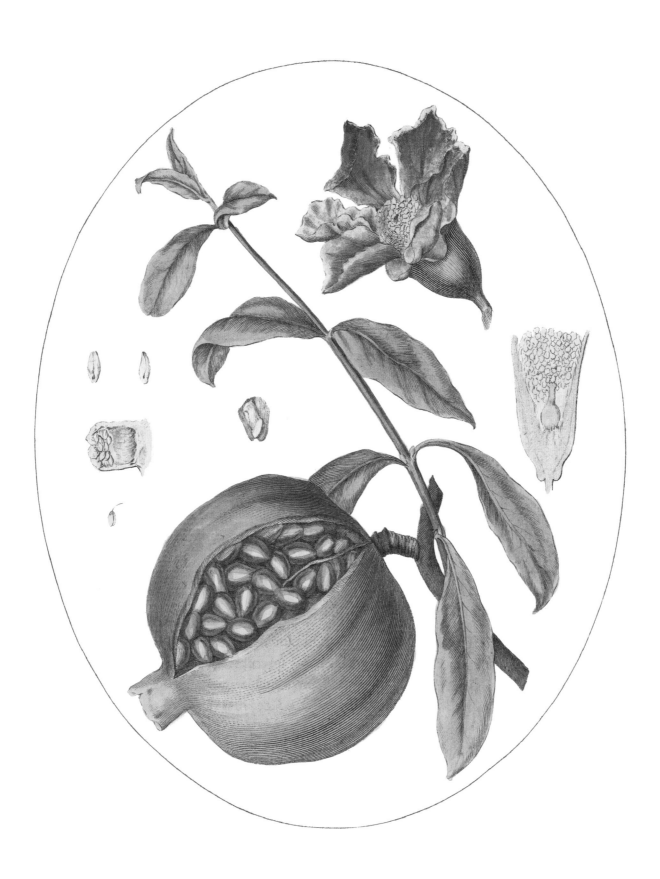

QUAILS

'Then a wind went out from the Lord and it brought quails from the sea and let them fall beside the camp, a day's journey on that side and a day's journey on the other side, all around the camp about two cubits deep on the ground.' NUMBERS 11:31

As Suyuti called quails 'victims of thunder', saying that if a quail heard thunder it would die. Although the *Coturnix coturnix* is a delicate little bird, thousands of quails successfully migrate from Central Europe to Africa every year. Many of the birds drop to the ground with exhaustion during the journey, sometimes carried by the wind. They fall on the beaches of the Holy Land and along the banks of the Nile. The gift of quails from the Lord, which saved the Hebrews from starvation, was most likely these migrating quails. Quail remains a popular food in the Holy Land. They can be enjoyed grilled, or, more elaborately, stuffed and roasted.

QUAIL WITH POMEGRANATE GLAZE

8 quails
125ml (½ cup) honey
125ml (½ cup) pomegranate concentrate,
60ml (4 tablespoons) vinegar
Salt and pepper

1. Rub the cleaned and prepared quails with salt and pepper.
2. To make the glaze, place the honey in a *bain-marie* (a mixing bowl balanced over a saucepan filled with a little boiling water). Whisk in the pomegranate concentrate and vinegar. Season with salt and pepper. Add a little water if necessary.
3. Generously glaze the birds, using a pastry brush. Place in a pre-heated oven at 180C (350F) for 15–30 minutes according to taste. Brush with any remaining glaze after the first 10 minutes of cooking. Serve hot or cold on a bed of green salad.

STUFFED QUAILS SYRIAN STYLE

8 quails
450g (1 pound) rice
8 tablespoons raisins
2 cooking apples, peeled and chopped
Salt and pepper

1. Boil the birds for 10 minutes, remove and throw away the water.
2. Rinse the rice using a sieve. Place in a saucepan of boiling salted water and cook for 10 minutes. Remove and drain. Mix in the raisins and chopped apple and season with salt and pepper.
3. Stuff the quails with the rice mixture. Place on a baking tray and surround with any left-over stuffing.
4. Cook in a pre-heated oven at 150C (300F) for 45 minutes. Serve hot along with stuffing.

QUAILS IN GRAPE SAUCE

8 quails
45ml (3 tablespoons) oil
60g (4 tablespoons) clarified butter
9cm (3 inches) fresh ginger, grated
1 garlic clove, crushed
450g (1 pound) green grapes
Salt and pepper

1. Place the grapes in a saucepan with the olive oil, season with salt and pepper, cover and cook over a low heat for 15 minutes.
2. Rub the cleaned and prepared quails with ginger, garlic, salt and pepper. Place in a pan with the butter and leave to cook for about 15 minutes, turning occasionally.
3. Pour the grapes over the quails and cook for 15 minutes. Serve hot.

PIGEON

Pigeon was enjoyed in ancient Egypt and it remains a national dish in Egypt to this day. The rock pigeon or squab was also present in the ancient Holy Land. *Columba palumbus* seems to have been domesticated about 3500 BC. The bird was first tamed for religious purposes; pigeon, for instance, was associated with the goddess Astarte in Mesopotamia. Homing pigeons were also used in classical times to transport the military messages of the Romans and even the Olympic Games results among Greek cities. Eventually, the bird began to be used as a food source. Pigeons are easily domesticated and must have been attractive in terms of husbandry in the ancient Levant owing to their serial breeding habits. Pigeon remains a popular fowl in the Levant but was overshadowed by chicken during the Byzantine period. Today, rock pigeons are about 3 times the size of the squabs of the ancient Holy Land.

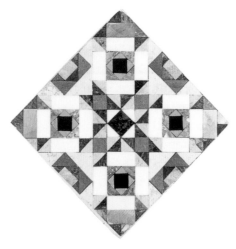

PIGEONS STUFFED WITH GREEN WHEAT

2 pigeons
200g (1 cup) (freekeh) green wheat

70g (½ cup) walnuts, chopped
2 small onions, peeled
Salt and pepper

1. Rinse the wheat in a colander, place in a saucepan and cover with water. Season, bring to the boil, and cook on a medium heat for 45 minutes.
2. Stir in the walnuts and season with salt and pepper.
3. Boil the pigeon for 10 minutes, remove and throw away the water.
4. Stuff the pigeons with the wheat and nut mixture. Seal the cavities of the birds with the onions.
5. Cook in a pre-heated oven at 200C (400F) for 1 hour. Serve carved, surrounded by the stuffing.

PARTRIDGE

'Now therefore, do not let my blood fall to the ground, away from the presence of the Lord; for the king of Israel has come out to seek a single flea, like one who hunts a partridge in the mountains.' SAMUEL 26:20

The word partridge actually refers to several plump-bodied game birds from Europe and Western Asia which belong to the genera *Perdix* and *Alectoris*. As the red-legged or rock partridge was widely hunted in the south of the Holy Land, partridge have been included in this book. Although not a common feature on today's table, it can be acquired through specialist butchers in major locations.

STUFFED PARTRIDGE

450g (1 pound) partridge
1 cabbage head, chopped
2 flat bread loaves, soaked in milk
100g (3 ½ ounces) goat's cheese
30ml (2 tablespoons) olive oil
1 carrot, cut into batons
1 onion, sliced
1 garlic clove, crushed
Salt and pepper

1. Break the milk-soaked bread into small pieces and combine with the goat's cheese, salt and pepper in a mixing bowl until they form a paste.
2. Fill the cavity of the cleaned and prepared bird with the paste. Place in a cold oven and set the temperature to 220C (440F).

After 30 minutes, baste the bird and adjust seasoning. Reduce the temperature to 200C (400F) and cook for another 1 hours 30 minutes, basting every 30 minutes.
3. Blanche the cabbage in boiling water for 10 minutes. Transfer to a dish with 30ml (2 tablespoons) of oil, the chopped carrot, onion, garlic, salt and pepper.
4. Serve the partridge accompanied by the cabbage and vegetables.

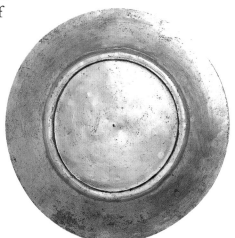

GOOSE

Geese were eaten by the Hebrews during their captivity in Egypt. They were often preserved in salt or in their own fat, which was prized for its delicate flavour. Although sometimes hunted in Egypt they were raised principally as a farm bird from the classical period onwards. It was the cackling of the geese of Rome that saved the city from attack. *Anser anser* were certainly preferred to duck and pigeon in the early Islamic period but As Suyuti saw their nutritional value as minor, saying, *'the heat of the goose is very great, its nutritional value lies halfway between good and bad'* [THE MEDICINE OF THE PROPHET, AS SUYUTI]. Goose has long been traditional Christmas fare in Europe, but has recently been replaced by the more affordable turkey in most households. Yet *foie gras d'oie,* or fatted goose liver, remains a prominent luxury food, especially in France.

STUFFED GOOSE

1.8kg (4 pounds) goose,
including liver
4 flat bread loaves
200g (7 ounces) goat cheese, crumbled
2 red onions, finely chopped
4 garlic cloves, crushed
1 parsley bouquet, finely chopped
125ml (½ cup) milk
Oil, to fry
Salt and pepper

1. Fry the goose livers with a little oil until browned. Season with salt and pepper and chop finely.
2. Break the bread in small pieces and combine with the chopped livers, cheese, garlic, onion, milk, in a mixing bowl until they form a paste. Adjust seasonings.
3. Fill the cavity of the cleaned and prepared bird with the paste.
Place in a cold oven and set to 220C (440F). After 30 minutes, baste the bird and adjust seasoning. Reduce the temperature to 200C (400F) and cook for another 2 hours 30 minutes, basting every 30 minutes. Serve hot.

MEAT

*'Every moving thing
that lives shall be
food for you ...'*

GENESIS 9:3

MEAT

DIETARY REQUIREMENTS

'They will come to you on foot and on the backs of swift camels from every distant quarter; they will come to avail themselves of many a benefit and to pronounce on the appointed days the name of God over the cattle which He hath given them for food. Eat of their flesh, and feed the poor and unfortunate.'

QURAN, THE PILGRIMAGE 22:26

There is no mention of flesh eating in the Bible until after the flood and even then the consumption of meat is severely restricted. Once meat eating is established, the Pentateuch lays out more guidelines and restrictions about eating meat than any other food. Within the tenets of the Christian faith there are few restrictions placed on the consumption of meat, yet Islam and Judaism outline strict guidelines about which types of meat can be consumed and how. Principally, both faiths prohibit the consumption of several 'unclean' animals. The book of Leviticus lists an array of animals that were forbidden to Moses and to the people of Israel, whilst the Quran outlines similar prohibitions for Muslims.

'But among those who chew the cud or have divided hoofs, you shall not eat the following; the camel … the rock badger … the hare … the pig … Of their flesh you shall not eat, and their carcasses you shall not touch; they are unclean for you.'

LEVITICUS 11:2–8

'You are forbidden carrion, blood, and the flesh of swine; also any flesh dedicated to any other than God. You are forbidden the flesh of strangled animals and of those beaten or gored to death; of those killed by a fall or mangled by beasts of prey (unless you make it clean by giving it the death stroke yourselves); also of animals sacrificed to idols.' QURAN, THE TABLE 5:3

Furthermore, the slaughter of those animals that are considered clean is regulated. The Hebrew scriptures specify that all life-blood must be drained from meat before it can be eaten. Over the centuries, traditions have emerged that regulate the practice of these food laws. Jewish food law requires that the animal be slaughtered in a ritual manner, which involves a fast, humane slitting of the throat. The meat is then examined for disease and is declared kosher. Jewish food law covers issues such as porging and an excerpt in the book of Exodus – *'You shall not boil a kid in its mother's milk'* [EXODUS 23 : 19] – has been interpreted by many Jews to mean that all mixing of dairy produce and meat is forbidden. Muslim food restrictions are not as complex as those of Judaism but in order for meat to be *halal*, or allowed, it must be slaughtered in a ritual manner where the throat is slit and the name of Allah is invoked.

'Only you shall not eat the flesh with its life, that is, its life-blood.' GENESIS 9:4

'He hath only forbidden you dead meat, and blood, and the flesh of swine, and that on which any other name hath been invoked besides that of Allah.' QURAN, THE COW 2:173

BARBECUES & GRILLING

Commonly, meat was patiently cooked over the burning embers of an open fire. Often, a pit was dug for the fire and a frame or spit erected . This method strongly resembles the *barbacoa* or barbecue of the Caribbean Amerindians that was later popularised by the cowboys of the United States. The lengthy cooking process makes for tender meat with a distinctive smoky flavour. Most barbecues that are widely available today are more like grills than pits. Any barbecue has to be thoroughly heated prior to cooking. Meat cooked in this way is still popular in the Arab world, where it is said to have been popularised by the Ottoman armies cooking meat on their swords on the battlefields. Indeed, flat metal skewers, similar to the Turkish swords, are by far the most effective implement when cooking meat in this way, as the hot metal heats the meat through and makes it easier to remove .

Generically, barbecued meats go under the name 'kebab' and are traditionally served with salad and parsley enveloped in flat bread. All different cuts and even whole animals were cooked in this way. They were balanced on a spit, laid out on a frame or simply placed in the embers. Meats were often marinated for several hours prior to cooking in order to make them tender, succulent and often aromatic. Certain animals, such as goats and gazelles, had to be heavily marinated in order to lessen their strong taste. Alternatively cuts were simply rubbed with spices before cooking.

MARINADES

TARRAGON MARINADE

125ml (½ cup) vinegar
125ml (½ cup) olive oil
2 tablespoons tarragon, chopped
1 teaspoon cumin
Juice of 1 lemon
Salt and pepper

GARLIC MARINADE

125ml (½ cup) vinegar
125ml (½ cup) olive oil
4 garlic cloves, crushed
Salt and pepper

PARADISE SPICE RUB

1 nutmeg
2 teaspoons black pepper-corns
2 teaspoons cloves
2 cinnamon sticks
3cm (1 inch) ginger, grated
1 teaspoon salt
1 teaspoon white pepper

MARINADE INSTRUCTIONS

1. Grind the spices into a fine powder using the pestle and mortar. To make the oil-based marinades, finely chop the ingredients and combine with the liquid.
2. Rub the dry spice or brush the marinade on the meat and leave to settle for 1–5 hours before cooking.

MUTTON & LAMB

'For the lamb in the midst of the throne shall feed them, and shall lead them unto living fountains of waters: and God shall wipe away all tears from their eyes.'
REVELATIONS 7:17

The most symbolic of all the animals mentioned in the Bible, lamb was the most common meat in the Holy Land and the preferred sacrificial offering. Many references to lamb in the spiritual texts are simply translated as 'meat'. Given that the girl's name Rachel means ewe, the Hebrews must have greatly valued their sheep. In the Christian tradition, lamb is a powerful metaphor for Jesus, the sacrificial vessel for the sins of mankind; *'Behold the lamb of God, who takes away the sins of the world'* [JOHN 1:29]. It remains an essential part of the Passover meal, and was probably eaten at the Last Supper. Sacrifice is considered an essential part of Islam and every year at the feast of *Id al-Adha,* each grown male is required to sacrifice a sheep as a symbol of his submission to God. Sheep had many uses in the Holy Land; their skin was used for roofing and clothing and their horns were used to make flasks. Moab, the Judean highlands and the hills of Syria were excellent environments in which to raise sheep. It seems that wild sheep, *Ovis orientalis,* were first domesticated about 8000 years ago in Central Asia and over the millennia made their way down to the Mediterranean, by which time they had evolved into *Ovis aries,* the common domesticated sheep.

Lamb remains the meat of choice in the Near East. In some areas, tallow, sheep tail fat, is still as prized in cooking as it was in ancient times. Broad-tailed sheep with tails so hefty that they were often rendered immobile were bred in biblical Palestine. Mutton was also enjoyed in ancient times, but lamb – sheep under one year without permanent teeth – were generally preferred to their stronger tasting, tougher and often otherwise useful elders. As with cows, size necessitated that sheep only be slaughtered when enough people were present to ensure all the meat was eaten. Today, the more tender lamb is preferred over mutton. Therefore these recipes have been composed with lamb in mind.

'It was related that Amr ibn Umaiya said : "My father said : I saw the Messenger of God (Muhammad) take a piece of cooked shoulder of mutton and then he was called for prayer."' SAYING OF MUHAMMAD, RELATED BY AL BUKHARI

BARBECUED LEG OF LAMB

'They shall eat the lamb that same night; they shall eat it roasted over the fire with unleavened bread and bitter herbs. Do not eat any of it raw or boiled in water.'
EXODUS 12:8–9

God instructed Moses and Aaron to commemorate the Passover by eating 'fire'-roasted lamb every year. Kosher butchers porge the sinews and veins from the hind leg of an animal. Ask a butcher to remove the bone from the leg and flatten the joint for this dish. A leg of lamb generally serves 8 unless the animal is very young, when it serves less.

1 boneless lamb leg
125ml (½ cup) oil
1 tablespoon chopped mint
1 tablespoon mustard
1 onion, finely chopped
3 garlic cloves
Salt and pepper

1. Combine the mint, mustard, onion, garlic, salt and pepper. Rub the mixture on the joint and leave to marinate for 2–4 hours.

2. Prepare a wood fire or barbecue, place the meat on a frame or on a spit over the embers. Turn the joint every 10 minutes. Rub with oil in order to prevent the meat from drying out.

MEAT WITH APRICOTS

Fruit and meat combinations were popular in Persia and Arabia. These dishes became common in Levantine cuisine following the Muslim conquest of the Holy Land. The apricots in this dish can always be substituted with plums.

450g (1 pound) lamb on the bone
450g (1 pound) apricots, peeled and de-seeded
Salt

1. Boil the meat for 10 minutes. Remove and throw away the water. Cover with fresh water and season with salt. Bring to the boil, cover, and cook for 1 hour. Reduce heat, and simmer for 1 hour.
2. Add the apricots and cook for another hour. Serve hot with rice.

PERSIAN LAMB AND DRIED FRUIT
STEW

450g (1 pound) shoulder of lamb
1 onion
65g (½ cup) yellow split peas, soaked
115g (4 ounces) prunes, soaked and
halved
115g (4 ounces) dried apricots,
quartered
65g (½ cup) pine nuts
Juice of ½ lemon
45ml (3 tablespoons) oil or clarified
butter
Salt and pepper

1. Remove any excess fat from the
meat and cut into cubes.
2. Gently fry the onion in the oil or
clarified butter until transparent,
season and set aside.
3. Fry the meat in the pan for 10
minutes. Return the onion to the pan
and add the split peas. Cover with
500ml (2 cups) of water, season and
bring to the boil.
4. Partly cover the pan, lower the heat
and cook for a further 30 minutes.
5. Add prunes, apricots and pine nuts
and leave on a low heat for 15–20
minutes. Stir in the lemon juice and
serve hot with rice.

MEAT AND QUINCE

450g (1 pound) shoulder of lamb
300g (10 ½ ounces) quince
125ml (½ cup) lemon juice or
pomegranate concentrate
2 tablespoons parsley, chopped
1 onion, chopped
Salt and pepper

1. Boil the meat for 10 minutes.
Remove and throw away the water.
Place the meat and onion in a
saucepan, cover with water and
season. Bring to the boil, and cook for
1 hour.
2. Peel and chop the quince. Add to
the pan and cook for another hour.
3. Just before serving, stir in the lemon
juice or pomegranate concentrate.
Add the parsley. Serve hot with rice.

ASPARAGUS WITH MEAT

This method of cooking minced lamb
with vegetables and lemon juice is
easy , nutritious and tasty. The asparagus can be substituted with other
vegetables such as chicory, or carrots.

200g (7 ounces) lamb, minced
450g (1 pound) asparagus, chopped
45ml (3 tablespoons) lemon juice
45ml (3 tablespoons) oil
Salt and pepper

1. Gently fry the meat in a large pan with clarified oil until browned. Stir in the chopped vegetables and cook for 5–10 minutes.
2. Season with salt and pepper and cover with water. Leave to simmer until well done.
3. Stir in the lemon juice and serve hot.

MEAT WITH POMEGRANATE SEEDS AND NUTS

450g (1 pound) shoulder of lamb, cubed
350g (12 ounces) minced lamb
1 large onion, cut into rings
300g (2½ cups) walnuts
200g (1½ cups) raisins
300g (10½ ounces) pomegranate seeds
2 teaspoons coriander
1 teaspoon cinnamon
1 teaspoon ginger, powdered
4 teaspoons dried mint
Salt and pepper

1. Boil the meat for 10 minutes. Remove and throw away the water.
2. Cover the meat with fresh water, season with salt, bring to the boil, reduce heat and cook for 30 minutes.
3. Grind all the spices together in a pestle and mortar. Add the pomegranate seeds, raisins and transfer to the pan.
4. Crush the nuts and add to the pan.

5. Season the minced meat and shape into walnut-sized meat balls . Add to the pan.
6. Cook on a medium heat for 1 hour or until the meat balls are tender. Serve hot.

ABRAHAM SPICED MEAT BALLS

450g (1 pound) lamb, chopped
1 tablespoon coriander, chopped
10 cm (4 inches) ginger root, peeled
1 teaspoon peppercorns
2 sticks cinnamon
2 medium onions, finely chopped
30ml (2 tablespoons) grape syrup
1 teaspoon vinegar
3 tablespoons almonds, toasted
1 teaspoon rose water
Salt

1. Boil the meat in water for 10 minutes. Remove and throw away the water. Cover with fresh hot water and season with salt. Bring to the boil, reduce heat and leave to simmer for 10 minutes.
2. Wrap the coriander, ginger, pepper and cinnamon in a piece of thin cloth or muslin and secure with string.
3. Add the parcel of herbs and the onions to the meat and leave to cook for another 10 minutes. Remove the meat and throw away the bag.

4. Mince the meat, shape into walnut-sized balls and return to the pan. Stir in the grape syrup and vinegar.
5. Cover and leave to simmer on an extremely low heat for 1 hour. Sprinkle with rose water and garnish with toasted almonds just before serving.

HONEYED LAMB

900g (2 pounds) shoulder of lamb, cubed
90ml (6 tablespoons) olive oil
1 medium onion, sliced into rings
450g (1 pound) raisins
65g (½ cup) almonds, chopped
250g (1 cup) honey
1 teaspoon saffron
½ teaspoon cumin
½ teaspoon thyme
½ teaspoon coriander
Salt and pepper

1. Heat the oil in a heavy-based pan, stir in the cumin, coriander, thyme, saffron and pepper.
2. Pour 250ml (1 cup) of water into the pan and leave to simmer on a very low heat for 5 minutes.
3. Add the onions and cubed meat to the pan. Leave to simmer until the meat becomes tender, adding more water if necessary.
4. Warm the honey and pour over the meat. Leave to simmer for about 5 minutes and add the raisins. Leave to simmer for another 20 minutes or until the sauce is reduced.
5. Toast the almonds and scatter over the meat and its sauce.

LAMB WITH BURGHUL

450g (1 pound) lamb on the bone
200g (7 ounces) burghul
5 cardamom pods
1 bay leaf
Salt
45ml (3 tablespoons) oil or clarified butter

1. Boil the lamb for 10 minutes. Remove and throw away the water. Cover with fresh water. Season with salt, add the bay leaf and cook on a medium heat for 2 hours.
2. Remove the meat, strain the cooking liquid and set both aside.
3. Rinse the burghul and drain in a sieve. Fry with the oil in a saucepan, stir continuously. Once the grains are coated, return the cooking liquid and the meat to the saucepan.
4. Bring the mixture to boil, reduce heat and leave to cook on a low heat until the liquid is absorbed. Serve hot.

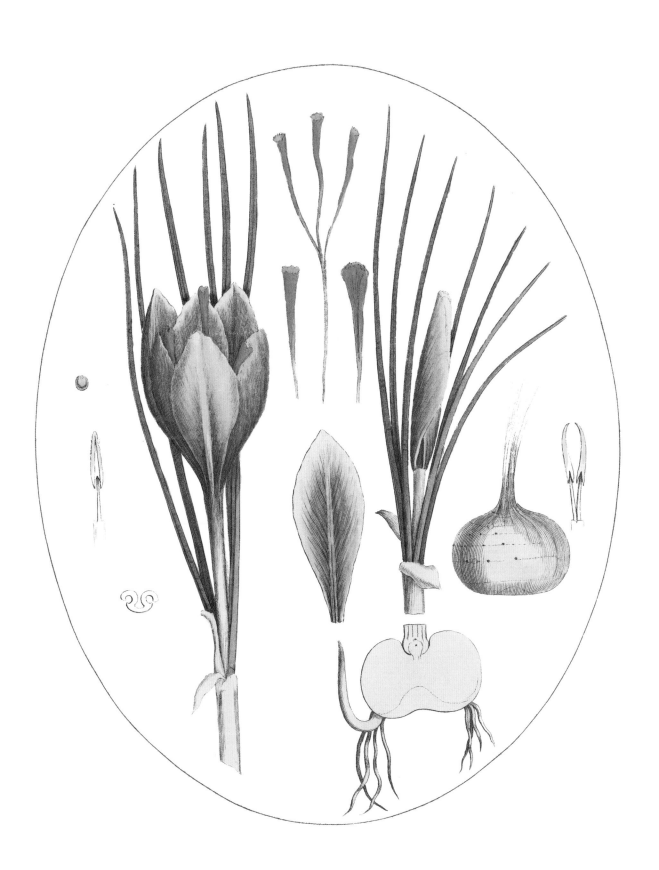

BAY LEAF

The bay leaf appears in the King James version of the Bible Psalms (37 : 35). But in later translations it is simply called 'green tree'. The bay leaf was particularly important in ancient Greco-Roman civilization. Apollo's love, Daphne, is supposed to have been enchanted in the tree. *Laurus nobilis* was traditionally used to crown the victorious in antiquity, and it still remains symbolic in the modern world where it lends its name to titles such as Poet Laureate. The bay leaf also remains a very important base note in Mediterranean cooking. Unlike other herbs, it is inedible and must be discarded before a dish is eaten.

BABYLONIAN BURIED LAMB

450g (1 pound) basmati rice
200g (7 ounces) fresh fava beans
4 bay leaves
90g (6 tablespoons) oil or clarified butter
300g (10 ½ ounces) lamb on the bone
Salt and pepper

1. Boil the meat for 10 minutes. Remove and throw away the water.
2. Cover with fresh water. Season with salt, bring to the boil, reduce heat and cook for 1 hour. Remove the meat, strain the cooking liquid and set both aside.
3. In a large pan, fry the fava beans with the oil for 5 minutes. Add the rice and cook for 5–10 minutes.
4. Add the meat and bury it at the bottom of the mixture. Add the bay leaves, cover with cooking liquid and secure the pan with a tight lid. Leave to cook on a low heat for 30 minutes, adding more cooking liquid or water if required.
5. Serve once the rice is tender, with the meat buried in the rice and fava beans.

PROPHET'S THARID

This broth is said to have been the
favourite dish of the prophet
Muhammad. He is said to have
compared his preference for the dish
to other foods to his preference for his
wife Ayesha to other women. The
meat is cooked for so long that it falls
away from the bone. As a variation
vegetables can be added to the pan
during the final hour of cooking.

450g (1 pound) burghul wheat
450g (1 pound) lamb on the bone,
such as the saddle
4 bay leaves
1 cinnamon stick
Salt and pepper

1. Boil the meat in water for 10
minutes. Remove and throw away
the water.
2. Rinse the wheat in a sieve and place
in a saucepan with the meat. Add the
bay leaves, cover with fresh hot water
and secure with a tight lid.
3. Cook on a very low heat for about
3 hours, or until all the liquid has been
absorbed. Serve hot.

VEAL

'Bring out the best robe, and put it on him; and put a ring on his hand, and shoes on his feet; and bring hither the fatted calf and kill it, and let us eat and make merry.'
LUKE 15:22–23

Throughout the Bible and the Quran, references to the fatted calf and the roasted calf indicate that it was the preferred animal for feasting. A calf, *'tender and good'* [GENESIS 18:6], has been a symbol of Hebrew hospitality since the time of the patriarch Abraham. The return of the prodigal son was a joyous occasion and merited a celebratory meal. The most common way to cook a calf in Holy Land feasts was to roast the whole animal over the burning embers of a wood fire. This is a slow process that could take up to a whole day. The calf was cleaned and prepared beforehand and then seasoned with salt and other spices. A calf was only slaughtered at large gatherings or special occasions.

VEAL WITH FRUIT

450g (1 pound) veal
300g (10 ounces) leeks, chopped
450g (1 pound) aubergines
150g (5 ounces) dates
130g (1 cup) almonds
30g (¼ cup) raisins
90g (3 ounces) dried figs
450g (1 pound) onions, chopped
45ml (3 tablespoons) vinegar
1 teaspoon ground coriander
1 teaspoon ground cinnamon
1 teaspoon saffron
1 teaspoon pepper
15ml (1 tablespoon) rose water
Salt and pepper

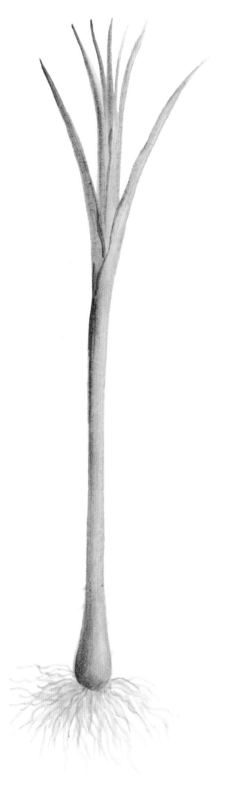

1. Cut the meat into small chunks and boil in water for 10 minutes. Remove and throw away the water. Cover the meat with fresh water, bring to the boil, reduce heat and leave to cook on a medium heat for 20 minutes. Remove the meat, strain the cooking liquid and set both aside.

2. Grind the coriander, salt and cinnamon with a pestle and mortar and sprinkle onto the meat with the saffron.

3. Peel and stone the dates and leave to soak in warm water.

4. Put all the above, along with the rest of the ingredients, in a large saucepan. Cover with the liquid from the meat and leave to simmer for 1 hour.

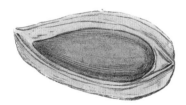

BEEF

'We have created for them the beasts of which they are masters. We have subjected these to them, that they may ride on some and eat the flesh of others; they drink their milk and put them to other uses.' QURAN, YA SIN 36:70

It seems that cattle were first domesticated about 8000 years ago in South Western Asia. *Bos taurus,* particularly the bull, stands out as an object of worship in the ancient world. The bull was regarded as sacred by many cults in Egypt. It was idolised by the early Hebrews and depictions of bulls appeared in temples as late as the reign of Solomon. A white bull was slaughtered at the *Feriae Latinae* in Rome every year. Beef was very rarely eaten in ancient times. Cattle were valued working animals and the source of dairy products, so it was their calves that were far more likely to be slaughtered for food. If a bull or cow was slaughtered, it would most likely to have been at a feast or a large gathering where there were enough mouths to eat the animal. As Suyuti did, however, recommend beef fat and the liquid yielded from ox shins for convalescents. But he added that beef was difficult to digest and that the animal was better eaten in the form of veal. Beef is rich in potassium compared to many other types of meat and is a good source of B vitamins, iron and protein. It is the most widely consumed red meat in the Western world today.

EMESSA STEW

450g (1 pound) veal or beef, minced
1 large aubergine, peeled and chopped
2 zucchini, chopped
1 onion, finely chopped
30ml (2 tablespoons) pomegranate concentrate
65g (½ cup) pine nuts
15ml (1 tablespoon) clarified butter or oil
Salt and pepper

1. Place the zucchini and aubergines in an oven dish and season with salt.
2. Fry the pine nuts in the clarified butter or oil until golden.
3. Mix the meat, onions, pomegranate

concentrate and pine nuts together and season. Shape the mixture into *kofta* (sausage shaped dumplings). Bind with an egg if necessary. Place on top of the vegetables in the oven dish.
4. Cover with 250ml (1 cup) of water and cook in a pre-heated oven at 200C (400F) for 50 mins. Adjust seasonings and serve hot.

MEAT WITH RAISINS

450g (1 pound) veal or shoulder of lamb
60g (½ cup) raisins
2 large onions
125ml (½ cup) honey
1 teaspoon saffron
2 teaspoons cinnamon
3 teaspoons ginger
Salt and pepper

1. Boil the meat for 10 minutes. Remove and throw away the water.
2. Cover with fresh water, add the ginger, saffron and season with salt. Bring to the boil, reduce heat and leave to cook for 10 minutes.
3. Add half of the honey and a sliced onion. Leave on a medium heat for 40 minutes or until the meat is tender. Remove meat and set aside.
4. Add the raisins and the remainder of the onions to the sauce and cook for another 5 minutes.

5. Transfer the meat to an oven dish and cover with the sauce. Pour the honey over the mixture.
6. Bake in a pre-heated oven at 180C (350F) for 10 minutes. The honey should caramelise but not burn. Serve hot, sprinkled with cinnamon and accompanied by rice.

KID GOAT

'So Gideon went into his house and prepared a kid, and unleavened cakes from an ephaph of flour, the meat he put in a basket and the broth he put in a pot, he brought them to him under the oak and presented them.' JUDGES 6:19

Goats are thought to be the first herd animal domesticated by man. Nine thousand years ago, *Capra hircus* were kept by Neolithic people in Iran and after a few millennia made their way to the Levant. Like cattle and sheep, goats were used in religious ceremonies and sacrificial rituals; the Mesopotamian god Enki was depicted with the head of a goat. Nearly every family in the Holy Land, no matter how poor, would have possessed at least one goat. The strong-tasting goat was the meat of the poor and also a valuable source of dairy produce. They were raised in herds with sheep but could also be found wild at En-Gedi and high up in the cliffs surrounding the Dead Sea. The prophet Muhammad is said to have thought that the best meat of the goat came from the fore-quarters. These recipes have been composed using kid meat, which according to As Suyuti is evenly balanced and easily digested. Today, kid meat is unpopular in Europe and North America but it is still eaten in the Near East and can make a surprisingly tasty dish.

KID STEW

900g (2 pounds) shoulder of kid, cubed
60ml (4 tablespoons) oil or clarified butter
200g (7 ounces) coarse burghul
2 cinnamon sticks
4 cloves
Salt and pepper

1. Brown the meat with half the oil on all sides. Cover with water and season with cinnamon, cloves, salt and pepper. Leave to simmer for 3 hours. Skim off any residue that forms. Remove the meat, strain the liquid and set both aside.
2. Rinse the burghul and place in a pan with the rest of the oil. Stir until the burghul is fully coated in fat. Cover with the meat stock from the pan,

bring to the boil, reduce heat and leave to simmer. Serve the kid meat and its sauce hot with burghul.

ROAST KID

1 kid goat
½ cup mint, finely chopped
2 tablespoons mustard
1 small onion, finely chopped
60ml (¼ cup) olive oil
60ml (¼ cup) vinegar
Salt and pepper

1. Combine the mint, mustard, onion, oil, vinegar, salt and pepper. Rub all over the kid, including inside the cavity. Leave to marinate for 1 hour.
2. Place in an oven dish in a pre-heated oven at 250C (500F) with 750ml (3 cups) of water. Cover with aluminium paper.
3. After 1 hour, lower the temperature to 150C, remove the aluminium paper. Baste the meat every 20 minutes for the remaining 2 hours.
4. Serve with vegetables and burghul.

KIBBEH

It is thought that the ancient Assyrians and Sumerians began to make kibbeh over four thousand years ago. Today, kibbeh is the national dish of Syria, Lebanon and Jordan. The preparation of kibbeh is considered an art form and the preserve of women. In the days before the modern food processor, women and girls spent long hours pounding and blending the meat and burghul together in a large stone pestle and mortar. Those with long, slim fingers were thought to be blessed as they could deftly make the most delicately shaped kibbeh. The word kibbeh (which describes these burghul and meat dumplings) actually means 'ball-shaped' in Arabic, yet kibbeh shells can be moulded into various forms.

KIBBEH PASTE

200g (7 ounces) fine burghul
200g (7 ounces) lean minced meat
Salt

1. Wash and rinse the burghul. Squeeze out excess water. Leave for 1 hour.
2. Remove any fat or gristle from the minced meat.
3. Blend the burghul with the minced meat and salt until it forms a paste.
4. Add water as required and mould the paste into the shape you require, keeping the mixture cool at all times. The kibbeh paste can be moulded into several different forms and stuffed or combined with sauces. Kibbeh are traditionally made with lamb but can be prepared with minced veal, venison, duck, goose or fish.

KIBBEH BALLS

450g (1 pound) kibbeh paste
Oil, to fry

1. Divide the kibbeh paste into balls of a size that can be contained in your fist. Make a hole in each ball with your finger. Rotate your finger until the ball is hollowed out and the walls are as thin as possible. Stuff the ball with filling or leave empty.
2. Purse the opening with your fingers and gently roll the ball in the palm of your hand to even out the ball into a round shape. The balls can be fried directly or parboiled and then fried.

KIBBEH TORPEDOES

450g (1 pound) kibbeh paste
Oil, to fry

1. Divide the kibbeh paste into balls of a size that can be contained in your fist. Make a hole in each ball with your finger. Rotate your finger until the ball is hollowed out and the walls are as thin as possible. Stuff the ball with filling or leave empty.
2. Purse the opening with your fingers and gently roll the ball in your hand or on a board into a torpedo shape.
3. The torpedoes can be fried directly or parboiled and then fried.

SPINNING TOP-SHAPED KIBBEH

450g (1 pound) kibbeh paste
200g (7 ounces) kibbeh filling
60g (4 tablespoons) clarified butter

1. Butter a baking tray and make the paste into thin flat discs (1cm thick) using a teacup.
2. Spoon the filling on to the centre of half of the discs. Cover each one with a corresponding disc. Press down the edges with wet fingers or a teacup to make spinning tops.
3. Butter the tops of the kibbeh and bake at 250C (500F) for 40 minutes.

TRIPOLI STUFFED KIBBEH

450g (1 pound) kibbeh paste
200g (7 ounces) kibbeh filling
60g (4 tablespoons) clarified butter
Pine nuts, to decorate

1. Lay out half of the kibbeh paste in a buttered baking tray. Cover the paste with an even layer of the filling.
2. Then cover with an even layer of the remaining kibbeh mixture.
3. Run a knife around the perimeter of the tray. Score into diamond shapes and decorate each with a pine nut.
4. Bake in a pre-heated oven at 200C (400F) for 30 to 40 minutes.

KATINA KIBBEH

200g (7 ounces) kibbeh paste
100g (3 ½ ounces) lamb, minced
65g (½ cup) pine nuts
90ml (6 tablespoons) oil or clarified butter

1. Fry the meat in half of the oil until slightly undercooked. Add the pine nuts and fry until golden.
2. For each kibbeh make 2 teacup-sized discs of paste. Smooth a layer of the filling mixture onto one and cover with the other to make a sandwich.
3. Press down the edges with wet fingers and mould each disc into a

hollowed ball. Roll on a board to get more spherical shapes. Fry in the remaining butter until golden brown, about 10 minutes.

MONK'S KIBBEH

200g (7 ounces) kibbeh paste
60g (½ cup) raisins
65g(½ cup) walnuts, chopped
2 onions, finely chopped
250ml (1 cup) olive oil

1. Gently fry the onion until golden in a little of the oil. Fry the walnuts separately until golden. Stir the walnuts and raisins into the onions. Combine and cook for several minutes. Pour the remainder of the oil over the mixture.
2. Stuff this mixture into spinning top kibbeh shells and brush the surface of each with any remaining oil.
3. Bake in a pre-heated oven at 250C (500F) for 40 minutes.

GOURD KIBBEH

200g (7 ounces) kibbeh paste
100g (3 ½ ounces) veal or lamb
1 onion, finely chopped
65g (½ cup) walnuts, chopped
300g (10 ½ ounces) gourd or squash, cubed
300g (10 ½ ounces) veal or lamb, cubed
100g (3 ½ ounces) chickpeas
1 teaspoon dried mint
Oil, to fry

1. Gently fry the onion with a little oil until golden, stir in the meat and walnuts and cook for several minutes.
2. Flatten the kibbeh paste into discs, spoon a little of the meat and nut mixture onto the centre of each one. Close the paste around the mixture like small parcels and roll in the palm of the hand until each form a small ball.

3. Place the cubed meat and the chickpeas in a pan, cover with water and bring to boil for 5 minutes. Add the gourd or pumpkin, mint and season with salt. Lower the heat and leave to cook for 40 minutes or until the meat and gourd are tender.
4. Add the kibbeh balls and cook for another 10 minutes on a medium heat. Serve hot.

YELLOW KIBBEH

400g (14 ounces) kibbeh paste
200g (7 ounces) lamb, minced
100g (¾ cup) pine nuts
2 teaspoons saffron
60g (4 tablespoons) clarified butter
Salt

1. Fry the pine nuts in butter until golden. Add the meat to the pan and fry until slightly undercooked.
2. Butter a baking tray and make the paste into thin flat discs (1cm thick) using a teacup.
3. Spoon the filling on to the centre of half of the discs. Cover each one with a corresponding disc. Press down the edges with wet fingers or a teacup to make spinning tops.
4. Butter the upper sides of the kibbeh and bake at 250C (500F) for 40 minutes. Serve hot.

SWINDLER'S KIBBEH

These kibbeh are often known as swindler's kibbeh as the eater may be tricked into thinking they contain meat. They do, however, make an excellent kibbeh recipe for vegetarians.

100g (½ cup) burghul
100g (½ cup) flour
2 onions, finely chopped
60ml (4 tablespoons) pomegranate concentrate
Salt
Olive oil, to fry

1. Wash and rinse the burghul, transfer it to a mixing bowl. Sieve the flour and a little salt into the mixing bowl.
2. Slowly drizzle water into the bowl and knead the mixture into a paste. Roll the paste into walnut-sized balls on a floured board. Place the balls in a saucepan, cover with salted water and boil for an hour.
3. Gently fry the onion in some oil until translucent, stir in the pomegranate concentrate.
6. Drain the kibbeh balls and add them to the onion and pomegranate mixture, simmer for another 10 minutes. Leave to cool and serve cold.

ALEPPO KIBBEH BALLS

200g (7 ounces) kibbeh paste
100g (3 ½ ounces) minced meat
65g (½ cup) toasted pine nuts
500ml (2 cups) stabilised cooking
yogurt
Juice of 2 lemons
2 teaspoons sesame paste
60g (4 tablespoons) clarified butter
or oil

1. Gently fry the pine nuts with half of
the butter. Set the nuts aside and add
the meat to the pan, brown and
combine with half of the nuts.
2. Make the paste into kibbeh balls
(see p. 289), stuff with the meat and
pine nut mixture and seal.
3. Boil the balls in salted water for
5 minutes. Transfer to a pan and fry in
clarified butter for a further 5 minutes.
Drain and set aside.
4. Mix the lemon juice, yogurt and
sesame seed paste in a saucepan. Season
with salt and gently heat the sauce
thoroughly without letting the
delicate mixture boil.
5. Arrange the kibbeh balls on a
serving platter and cover with the
yogurt sauce. Garnish with remaining
pine nuts and serve hot.

KIBBEH IN APRICOT SAUCE

200g (7 ounces) kibbeh paste
200g (7 ounces) apricots
Oil, to fry
Salt and pepper

1. To make the apricot syrup: chop
fresh apricots and place them in a
saucepan with all their juices. Bring to
the boil, reduce heat, cover and cook
on a medium heat for 1 hour. If using
dry apricots, finely chop, place them
in a saucepan, cover with water and
cook on a medium heat for 1 hour.
Pass the cooked apricots through a
sieve and discard any fibrous material.
2. Make the paste into kibbeh balls
(see p. 289). Fry the balls in oil until
crisp on the outside.
3. Bring the apricot syrup to the boil
and season with salt and pepper.
Reduce heat and leave to simmer for
about 5 minutes.
4. Add the kibbeh balls to the syrup
and cook for another 5 minutes.
Serve hot.

Descent upon the Valley of the Jordan

DESSERTS

'He will take your daughters to be
perfumers and cooks and bakers.'

I SAMUEL 8:13

FRUIT

'Such is the paradise which the righteous have been promised. Therein shall flow rivers of water undefiled, and rivers of milk forever fresh; rivers of wine delectable to those that drink it, and rivers of clarified honey. There they shall eat of every fruit and receive forgiveness from their Lord.' QURAN, MUHAMMAD 47:15

As sugar cane refinement in the ancient world was primitive and labour-intensive, people relied on fruit and, to a lesser extent, honey as their principal sweeteners. Fruit was a highly valued and much appreciated food. This is reflected in the fact that fruit, particularly grapes, olives, figs, dates and pomegranates, merited extensive mention throughout the spiritual texts. Modern medicine tells us that fructose, the sugar found in fruit, is a far healthier alternative to sucrose and glucose, which are commonly consumed in their refined forms. Several of today's illnesses, such as obesity and diabetes, are seriously aggravated by the over-consumption of refined sugar. Therefore, it is possible that the people of the ancient world were fortunate that the sugar in their diet was so limited. Fruit is also packed with essential nutrients, notably vitamin C. Muhammad recommended fruit to convalescents and pregnant women, particularly dates and figs. The Mediterranean climate meant that an enormous variety of fruit thrived in the Holy Land. As well as eaten raw, fruit was cooked and preserved in several different ways in the ancient Levant. It was dried, boiled and pressed to make jellies, jams, pastes, cakes, syrups and juices. Organically grown fruits are recommended for the recipes in this book whenever possible.

FIG

'And the stars of the sky fell to the earth as the fig tree drops its winter fruit when shaken by a gale.' REVELATIONS 6:13

Most common in the mountainous areas of Palestine, *Ficus caprica* were often cultivated in small groups in the corner of vineyards. In ancient times they were fertilized by a process of caprification, which involved the rubbing of their boughs against one another. Otherwise, they relied on the wind and the tiny fig fly for their pollination. 'Early figs', most of which are blown to the ground, are prized for their flavour, yet the main crop of 'late figs' is usually in August. Fig leaves are probably best remembered for having scantily clothed Adam and Eve in the garden of Eden. Notably, the ninety-fifth book of the Quran is titled *'Al Tin'* or 'the fig' and opens with the words, *'By the fig and by the olive, by Mount Sinai and by this inviolate city'* [QURAN, THE FIG 95:1]. Figs were certainly a popular fruit in Biblical times when they were eaten either fresh, dried, or made into cakes or sweet juice. Figs are renowned for their healing properties. Pliny recommended them for convalescents and Muhammad believed that they could alleviate piles and gout. Modern science confirms that they have laxative and anti-bacterial properties, and can help relieve ulcers. *'Then Abigail hurried and took two hundred loaves, two skins of wine, five sheep ready dressed, five measures of parched grain, one hundred clusters of raisins, and two hundred cakes of figs'* [1 SAMUEL 25:18].

FIG CAKES

375g (1½ cups) dried figs
65g (½ cup) almonds, chopped
65g (½ cup) pistachios,
2 teaspoons cinnamon
125ml (½ cup) double cream

1. Soak the figs in warm water for 2 hours. Drain and chop finely.
2. Toast the almonds and place in a bowl with the pistachios, figs and cinnamon. Mix well.
3. Spoon the mixture into mounds onto an oiled baking tray. Use 2 dessert spoons to shape the mounds.
4. Bake in a pre-heated oven at 180C (350F) for 15 minutes. Eat with cream.

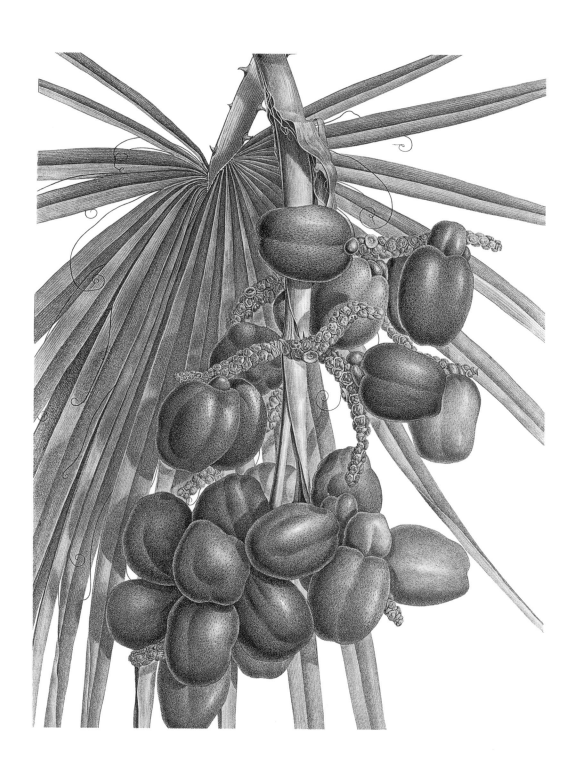

DATE

'We send down blessed water from the sky with which We bring forth gardens and the harvest grain, and tall clusters of dates, a sustenance for men; thereby giving new life to a dead land. Such shall be the Resurrection.' QURAN, 50:9

The date palm tree grew all over the Near East and was very important, not just because of the fruit it bore but because the leaves and bark could also be used as roofing or fuel. *Phoenix dactilifera* is the oldest food plant known to man and archaeological evidence of date palm seeds dating back 50,000 years has been found in the Shandihar cave of Northern Iraq. The Sumerians began to cultivate dates about 5000 BC. Dates were probably the most widely consumed fruit in the ancient Levant and remain deeply associated with Judaism, Islam and Christianity. As well as yielding the popular fruit, the palm tree was also used for shelter and to make ropes and construction materials. Dates were the main source of sugar in the ancient Levant, often eaten in some unusual combinations: *'I saw the Prophet eat fresh dates with cucumber'* [LIFE OF MUHAMMAD RELATED BY ABD ALLAH IBN JA'FAR BIN ABI TALIB, IN AL BUKHARI]. Dates are recommended in the Hadith as the food with which to break the fast, as they are wholesome but not so rich as to upset the stomach. Muhammad also recommended that they be eaten for breakfast. This is probably because they are a good source of energy as well as providing reasonable amounts of iron and calcium.

HALWA WITH DATES

140g (1 cup) wholemeal flour
250g (1 ½ cups) dates, crushed
15ml (1 tablespoon) sesame oil
2 teaspoons cardamom, ground
125g (½ cup) clarified butter
1 teaspoon cinnamon
65g (½ cup) assorted nuts, chopped

1. Melt the butter in a pan and gently brown the flour and cardamom.
2. Transfer half of the mixture to a baking tray. Spread a layer of the paste on the tray, cover with a layer of crushed dates and follow with a layer of the remaining paste. Place the mixture in the refrigerator for at least 6 hours and decorate with the nuts.

SMOKED DATE SANDWICH

180g (1 ½ cups) roasted flour
70g (½ cup) white flour
375ml (1 ½ cups) whole milk
1 tablespoon yeast
2 eggs
250g (1 cup) butter
1 teaspoon cardamom, ground
750g (3 cups) dates, crushed

1. Place the flour in a baking dish and gently roast in the oven for 20 minutes to get a smoked flavour. If using dry yeast, dissolve in a little water.
2. Sieve the roast flour, the plain white flour and the ground cardamom into a mixing bowl. In a separate bowl beat the eggs, milk, yeast and butter together. Make a well in the centre of the flour and pour in the liquid. Blend the 2 mixtures, cover with a damp cloth and leave to stand for 20 minutes.
3. Spread a 3cm (1 inch) thick layer of the paste in a baking dish. Cover with a layer of the chopped dates and follow with a layer of the remaining paste.
4. Place in a pre-heated oven at 180C (350F) and cook for 20 minutes.

MAMOUL

20 dates, pitted
450g (1 pound) semolina flour
70g (½ cup) plain white flour
170g (⅔ cup) clarified butter
125g (½ cup) sugar
15ml (1 tablespoon) orange flower water
15ml (1 tablespoon) rose water
125ml (½ cup) water
½ tablespoon yeast

Alternative filling
260g (2 cups) pistachios
30g (2 tablespoons) sugar
1 teaspoon orange flower water

1. Place the semolina, flour, sugar and butter in a mixing bowl and knead into a paste. Add in the rose water, orange blossom essence, warm water and yeast.
2. Cover and leave in a warm place for about 6 hours.
3. If filling with the pistachio mixture: mix the pistachios, sugar and orange blossom water together in a bowl.
4. Separate the mixture into small balls. Flatten into discs, spoon filling on to half the discs and cover with remaining discs, seal with fingers.
4. Place in a pre-heated oven at 150C (300F) for 15 to 20 minutes. Roll mamoul in sugar before serving hot or cold.

HONEY

'Your Lord inspired the bee, saying: "Make your homes in the mountains, in the trees, and in the hives which men shall build for you. Feed on every kind of fruit, and follow the trodden paths of your Lord." From its belly comes forth a syrup of different hues, a cure for men. Surely in this there is a sign for those who would take thought.'
QURAN, THE BEE 16:68

Honey is frequently mentioned in the spiritual texts, indicating the extent to which it was valued by ancient people. It was often given as a gift in biblical times [GENESIS 43:11; KINGS 14:3], and is a salient feature in all visions of Paradise. In Assyria, honey was even poured over the bolts of temples and sacred buildings. The liquid extracted from *Apis mellifera* was the preferred sweetener in the ancient world. The early Hebrews collected wild honey from rocks and trees, in contrast to the Egyptians, who practised bee-keeping in lower Egypt, which was commonly known as 'Bee Land'. Honey has antibacterial, tranquillising and anti-depressive properties. Muhammad, who is said to have been partial to honey and sweet things, realized the healing quality of honey and said, *'You have two medicines: honey and the Quran'* [SAYING OF MUHAMMAD RELATED BY AS SUYUTI]. Similarly, it is reported that the prophet drank a cup of honey with warm water on an empty stomach every day to preserve his health.

HONEY AND SESAME TREATS

250ml (1 cup) honey
½ teaspoon lemon juice
125g (1 cup) sesame seeds
65g (¼ cup) almonds, chopped
1 teaspoon sesame seed paste (tahina)

1. Slowly bring the honey to the boil in a pan over a medium heat.

2. Add the lemon juice, leave to boil for 1 minute and reduce the heat.
3. Toast the sesame seeds in a pan over a low heat until lightly brown.
4. Add toasted sesame seeds and chopped almonds to the honey. Briefly boil again, remove from heat.
5. Grease a tray with sesame seed paste. Pour in the mixture, cool until brittle then cut into squares to serve or store.

MYRTLE

'I will plant in the wilderness the cedar, the shittah tree, and the myrtle, and the oil tree ...' ISAIAH 41 : 19

Myrtus communis is a popular, wild highland shrub that was cultivated in the Holy Land gardens for its delicate white flowers and aromatic, edible berries. This sweet-scented shrub was dedicated to Venus in the classical world. Myrtle was also held in high esteem by Muhammad, whom As Suyuti is reported to have said, 'If anyone offers you myrtle as a present do not refuse it, for it comes from the Garden [of Eden].' It was even thought to be the queen of sweet smelling shrubs and was said to have been one of the three plants that Adam brought with him from the Garden of Eden. It was mainly appreciated for its scent but was also made into jelly, baked into cakes and its berries dried to be used as a spice.

MYRTLE TART

140g (1 cup) plain flour
15ml (1 tablespoon) fresh yeast
½ teaspoon salt
45g (3 tablespoons) butter
30g (2 tablespoons) sugar
1 egg, beaten
180ml (⅔ cup) warm milk
1 tablespoon olive oil
450g (1 pound) fresh myrtles
Icing sugar, to cover
Cream, to serve

1. Sieve the flour into a mixing bowl with the salt and make a well in the centre. Dissolve the yeast in 1 tablespoon of warm water.
2. Pour the sugar, warm milk, oil, beaten egg and yeast into the flour well. Combine the ingredients in the bowl until they acquire a dough-like consistency. Transfer the dough to a floured board and knead until smooth.
3. Cover the dough with a warm damp cloth and leave to stand for 30 minutes. Roll out the dough to fit a greased cake tin, press down firmly and leave to stand for another 20 mins.
4. Place a layer of the berries on the dough and transfer to a pre-heated oven at 250C (500F) to cook for 20 minutes. Sieve a layer of icing sugar over the tart. Serve cool with cream.

NUTS

'I went down to the nut orchard ...' SONG OF SOLOMON 6:11

Nuts were enjoyed in biblical times as food, flavouring and gifts. Although nuts are laborious to collect and prepare, their nutritional benefits are considerable. They are a rich source of protein and essential fatty acids as well as being conveniently compact packages of energy, due to their high calorie content. In addition to the almond and walnut, popular Holy Land nuts included the pistachio (*Pistachia vera*), a valuable and strikingly green nut which is typically used in confectionery. The most prized pistachios were said to be found in Aleppo. The similarly expensive pine nut (*Pinus pinea*) was also common in the Levant, as were the chestnut (*Castania sativa*) and hazelnut (*Corylus avellina*).

NUT SOUP

140g (1 cup) rice flour
400g (2 cups) sugar
1 tablespoon cinnamon
1 ½ litres (6 cups) water
65g (½ cup) pine nuts
65g (½ cup) walnuts
65g (½ cup) toasted almonds

1. Place the rice flour in a saucepan, cover with water and cook on a low heat for 10 minutes. Add the sugar and cinnamon to the pan, bring to the boil, reduce heat and leave to simmer for 30 minutes. Toast the nuts separately.
2. Divide out the nuts into single serving bowls and cover each with the rice syrup. Serve hot.

MAMOUNIA

200g (1 cup) semolina
90g (6 tablespoons) butter
60g (4 tablespoons) honey
750ml (3 cups) milk
½ teaspoon cinnamon
65g (½ cup) almonds, chopped

1. Melt the butter in a pan and gently fry the semolina. Slowly pour in the milk and stir in the honey. Cook on a medium heat for 15 minutes while stirring continuously.
2. Transfer to a serving dish and sprinkle with cinnamon and almonds.

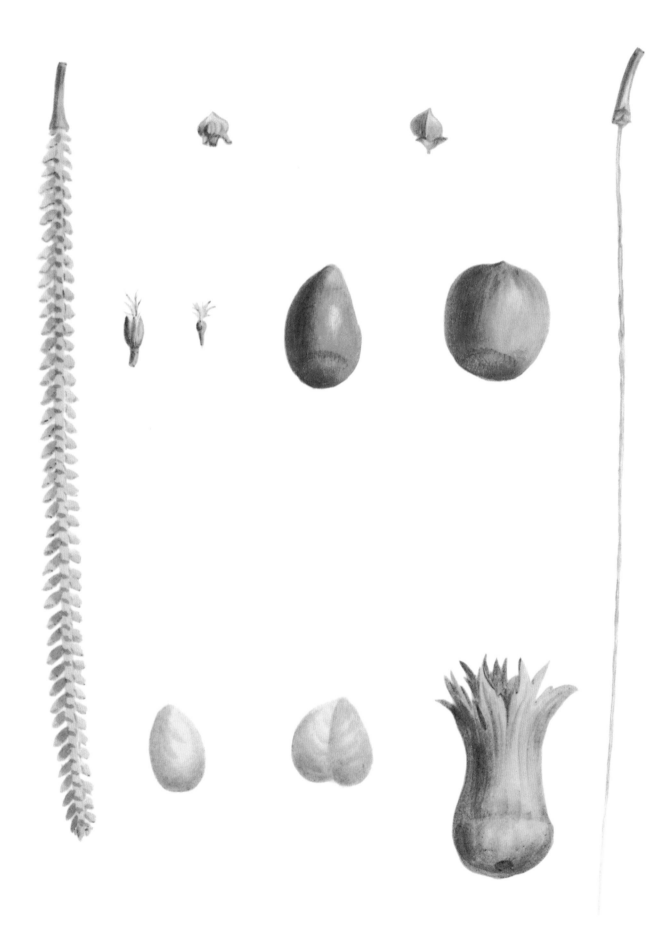

WALNUTS

'Cheese is a disease and walnuts are a medicine. If you combine the two then you have a remedy.' SAYING OF MUHAMMAD RELATED BY AL WASILA, IN AS SUYUTI

It is said that the Prophet Muhammad was particularly partial to walnuts. *Juglans regia*, the common Persian walnut, grows wild in the Northern Mediterranean basin and has been gathered since ancient times. As well as having a very distinctive bitter flavour, walnuts can also be ground down to a paste which was used to dye garments. Additionally, the walnut tree was used to make furniture; to this day it remains a very desirable wood. Walnuts contain considerable amounts of protein and unsaturated oil, particularly the linoleic and oleic varieties. Ripe walnuts contain vitamin E and the younger nuts contain some vitamin C.

HAROSET

This fruit and nut compote was an important element in the Passover meal. It symbolised the stones that Hebrew slaves used to build the pyramids of Egypt.

'And their father Israel said to them, "If it must be so, then do this: take some of the choice fruits of the land in your bags, and carry them down as a present to the man – a little balm and a little honey, gum, resin, pistachio nuts, and almonds."' GENESIS 43:11

65g (½ cup) dates, pitted
65g (½ cup) dried apricots, pitted
65g (½ cup) dried figs
30g (¼ cup) walnuts, chopped
30g (¼ cup) pistachios, chopped
30g (¼ cup) almonds, chopped
1 teaspoon cinnamon
½ teaspoon ginger
65ml (¼ cup) lemon juice

1. Soak the fruit in water for 2 hours. Drain well and chop roughly. Place in a pan and heat for 10–15 minutes.
2. Transfer to a storage vessel and mix with the chopped nuts, cinnamon, ginger and lemon juice. Serve with fresh fruit.

MULBERRY

'You shall not go up after them; go around and come on them opposite the balsam trees. When you hear the sound of marching in the tops of the balsam trees, then go out to battle; for God has gone out before you to strike down the army of Philistines.'
II SAMUEL 5:23

Scholars agree that the balsam mentioned in the above quote is actually mulberry. Mulberries were grown in ancient Palestine, as they are today, for their fruit. *Morus nigra* probably originated in Iran and was known to the ancient Egyptians, Greeks and Romans. When combined with sugar, honey and spices, mulberry juice makes a delicious drink, which is still popular in the region today. Mulberry jelly was used to alleviate sore throats in ancient times. The berries are a good source of potassium and vitamin C.

MULBERRY CANDY

250g (1 cup) mulberries
400g (2 cups) sugar
30g (2 tablespoons) butter

1. Place the mulberries in a saucepan and cook on a low heat until soft. Pass the berries through a sieve to extract 180ml (⅔ cup) juice.

2. Place the mulberry juice, sugar and butter in a pan and cook on a very low heat, stirring gently. Leave the mixture to settle and bring to the boil.
3. Remove the mixture from the heat and set aside to cool a little. Break it up with a wooden spoon and beat lightly.
4. Transfer to moulds or spread out in a tray and cut into diamond shapes. Leave to harden before eating.

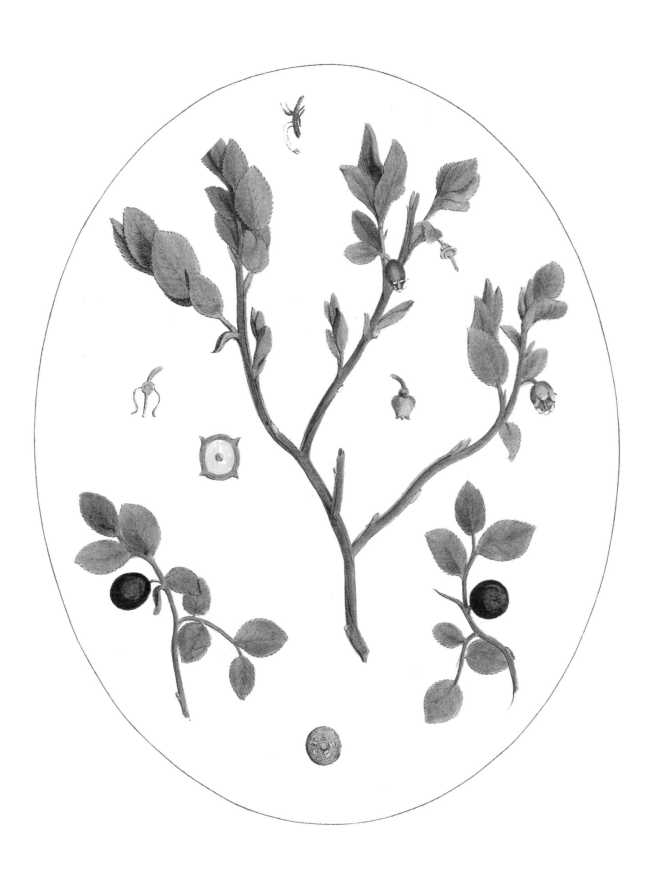

APPLE

'As an apple tree among the trees of the wood, so is my beloved among young men. I sat down under his shadow with great delight, and his fruit was sweet to my taste... Comfort me with apples ...' SONG OF SOLOMON 2:3,5

Although there are many references to apples throughout the Bible, there is speculation as to whether the 'apple' of the Bible is not, in actual fact, the 'golden apple' of Greece: the apricot. However, several scholars maintain that the apple had already appeared in Biblical times. Apples are mentioned in Hittite law codes and were therefore most likely distributed by Hittite traders in the Holy Land. What is certain is that the apples of the ancient Levant were nothing like the cultivated apples we know today. Today's species of apples descend form *Malus sylvestris*, a wild variety which has been grafted every century since the time of the Greeks to produce what we know as apples. The apples of ancient times were recognised as beneficial to health on account of, among other things, their anti-bacterial and antiviral properties. They are also a good source of potassium and vitamin C.

FRUIT SALAD

2 apples
2 bananas
4 peaches
1 medium-sized bunch of grapes
4 fresh figs
30g (¼ cup) raisins
60ml (4 tablespoons) honey
30ml (2 tablespoons) orange blossom essence
4 walnuts, chopped

1. Halve the grapes and remove the pips. Wash, peel and chop all the remaining fruits and nuts.
2. Place the fruit in a serving bowl with their juices. Add the orange blossom extract , the honey, the raisins and chopped nuts. Leave to stand for 1 hour before serving cold.

SUGAR CANE

'You have not bought me sweet cane with money ...' ISAIAH 43:24

Sugar cane is thought to have originated in the South Pacific island of New Guinea about 8000 years ago. *Saccharum officinarum* slowly spread westward and reached Northern India where it was discovered by Alexander the Great. Cane sugar was certainly known in biblical times but it remained a rare and expensive luxury. A process of extracting granulated sugar existed, but it was a primitive and labour-intensive process; the cane, therefore, was mainly enjoyed in its natural state. It was not until the discovery of this 'Persian reed' by Muhammad and his armies that sugar cane began to flourish. Following the Muslim conquests, sugar cane spread throughout the Mediterranean, but still, honey remained the preferred sweetener throughout the Near East. According to As Suyuti, whoever sucks some sugar after his meals will be happy for the whole day. Muhammad recognised the dangers of eating too much sugar, warning that the reed would cause tooth decay if it were used to clean teeth, as other reeds were at the time. Today, much of our sugar comes from sugar beet as well as sugar cane, which can also be found in liquid form. Refined sugar consumption has increased dramatically in recent times. Sugar is often a hidden ingredient in many supposedly savoury, packaged foods. Excessive sugar consumption leads to weight gain, lethargy and can prove a catalyst for diabetes. However, a small amout of sugar can aid digestion or help recovery after a shock.

RICE PUDDING

1 litre (4 cups) whole milk
200g (1 cup) pudding rice
100g (½ cup) sugar
15ml (1 tablespoon) orange blossom essence
Green pistachios, to decorate

1. Place the rice in a saucepan of boiling water and slowly cook until it absorbs the water. Pour in the milk, bring to the boil, reduce heat and simmer for 60 minutes.
2. Add the sugar to the pan, bring to the boil, reduce heat and simmer for 5 minutes.

3. Mix a little orange blossom essence into the mixture and divide into single serving bowls. Leave to cool and sprinkle with green pistachios before serving.

FESTIVE HALWA

375ml (1 ½ cups) water
75g (½ cup) rice flour
50g (¼ cup) sugar
125g (½ cup) semolina
100g (3 ½ ounces) white cheese, such as mozzarella
30ml (2 tablespoons) orange blossom water

1. Bring the water to the boil in a pan and pour in the rice, leave to cook for about 5 minutes. Add the sugar and leave to dissolve for 5 minutes before adding the semolina.
2. Bring to the boil, stirring vigorously. Add the orange blossom water and the thinly sliced mozzarella to the pan and work into the mixture, lifting it upwards with a wooden spoon until it acquires an elastic texture and the cheese has melted.
3. Spread a thin layer of the mixture on a serving platter and leave to cool.
4. This dessert can be eaten simply as it is, decorated with flower petals or smeared with double cream and rolled.

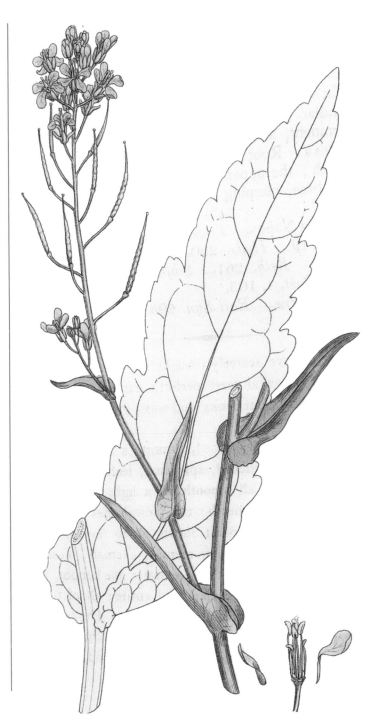

CAROB

The Carob tree, or *Ceratonia siliqua,* is native to the Near East. Its pods are lined with a soft brown pulp and are often used as a natural sweetener and chocolate substitute. Commonly known as St. John's bread, it is still unclear whether the 'locust' on which John the Baptist survived during his forty days in the wilderness is carob or the insect. It was well known to the Greeks and is believed to have been eaten by Muhammad's army during their campaigns. As Suyuti said that the staff of Suleyman was made from the wood of the tree. Carob is a nutritious fat-free alternative to chocolate. Therefore its pods are roasted and broken into kibble, a product which can be eaten by diabetics. A thick syrup known as *dibbs kharoub* is extracted from the pod in the Holy Land.

CAROB CAKE

250ml (1 cup) honey
45g (3 tablespoons) clarified butter
4 eggs
250ml (1 cup) milk
300g (2 ½ cups) whole wheat flour
3 tablespoons cinnamon
4 tablespoons carob powder
½ teaspoon salt

1. Beat the warmed honey and clarified butter together in a bowl. Slowly mix in the eggs and finally the milk.
2. Sieve the flour into a separate bowl and combine with the cinnamon, salt and carob powder.
3. Make a well in the centre of the dry mixture and slowly pour in the liquid, combine the 2 mixtures well.
4. Place in a cake tin and transfer to a pre-heated oven at 180C (350F) and bake for 35 minutes.

BEVERAGES

*'But those who drink
the water I give will become in
them a spring of water gushing
up to eternal life.'*

JOHN 4:14

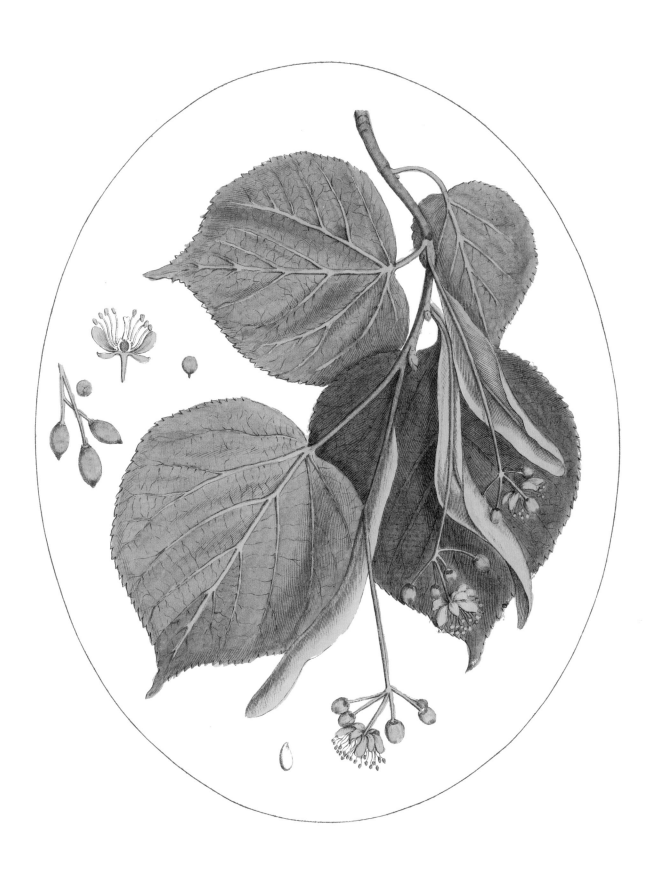

INSPIRED
EATING

Man does not live by bread alone,
but by every word that comes from
the mouth of God.'

MATTHEW 4:4

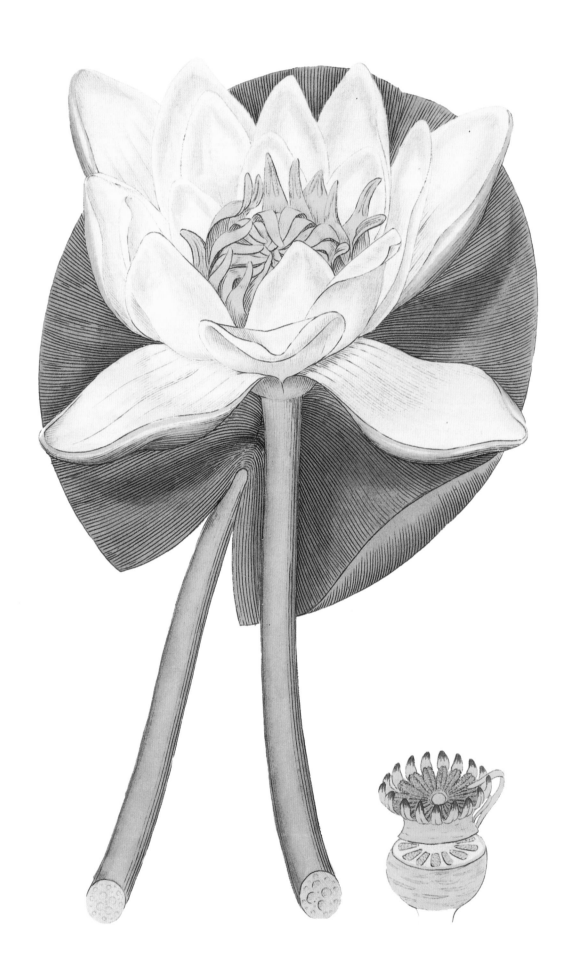

INSPIRED EATING

While the food we eat is vitally important for our general health, it is not enough on its own to ensure true and complete well-being. In order to make sure that we reap the maximum spiritual and physical benefits of our diet, the whole issue of how best to eat needs to be addressed. Only by taking a holistic approach to food can we hope to fully achieve a healthy, balanced lifestyle. The spiritual texts are peppered with advice and hints about how we should go about 'inspired eating'.

The Islamic texts are particularly rich in this respect, but there are many subtle pointers in the Bible. The Hadith, the collected sayings of Muhammad, is packed with information about eating as part of an all-round spiritual lifestyle. In addition to matters that have a direct bearing on health, there is also a considerable amount of information on etiquette and protocol. For example, it is wise not to criticise food offered to you by others, merely leave that which you do not like. Similarly, it is polite to eat the food nearest you rather than reaching across the table. If one sifts through the spiritual texts there is a large body of advice about how to eat in a way that promotes physical and spiritual well-being.

FASTING

'It was related that Abu Huraira said that the Messenger of God said that God Almighty said: "Every deed of the son of Adam is for himself, except for fasting which is for Me, and I will reward for it."' SAYING OF MUHAMMAD RELATED BY AL BUKHARI

Just as eating and sharing food is a central element of the three major monotheistic religions, so too is fasting. For Muslims the Ramadan fast, or *Sawm*, is considered so important that it comprises one of the 5 pillars of Islam. During Ramadan, which falls on the ninth month in the Islamic calendar, Muslims fast from sunrise to sunset. Illustrious figures in Islam, such as Caliph Omar, were avid fasters. Jews annually fast on the day of Yom Kippur, the Day of Atonement. Although modern Christians do not have similarly rigid traditions of fasting, it was certainly an important and admired activity in the Bible; *'Blessed are those who hunger and thirst for righteousness, for they shall be satisfied'* [MATTHEW 5:6]. Many Christians still forgo certain foods during Lent, the traditional period of xerophagy which falls between Ash Wednesday and Easter Sunday in remembrance of Jesus' forty days in the desert. Some still undergo sustained periods of fasting and refrain from eating meat on Fridays and in the hours before receiving Communion.

An important element in the holistic approach to eating, fasting can be beneficial for both physical and mental well-being. On a physical level it is widely believed that it gives the body a chance to rest and cleanse itself. It allows us to distinguish between hunger and cravings. This age-old thinking is now reflected by new-age health movements, which advocate fasting and detoxification diets. More significant than the physical advantages, however, are the mental and spiritual benefits. It is believed that by cleansing the human system, we can become more receptive to God. Fasting provides a chance for us to take stock and detach ourselves from our physical state and thus become less spiritually inhibited. Additionally, it reminds us

of our dependence on God and each other. As with feasting, fasting often brings religious communities closer, as both rich and poor share in the same experience. It can help people who normally eat well to remember what it feels

like to be hungry, and so can prompt privileged members of society to think of their less fortunate brothers and sisters. More importantly, fasting, like prayer, affords us an opportunity to reflect upon the food we eat and consequently make improvements where necessary.

Although fasting is certainly beneficial, it is not an activity to be undertaken lightly. Productive and safe abstinence requires a certain amount of planning and consideration. Extreme fasting over sustained long periods of time can be dangerous. Each faster needs to carefully consider his or her physical limitations. Certain people should take extreme caution or not fast at all. They include the old, the sick, travellers, pregnant or nursing mothers, young children and some adolescents. Abstainees should take great care to sleep well and avoid exertion. Foods used to break the fast should be carefully chosen so as not to shock the system. Muhammad recommended that the fast be broken with fresh dates and, failing that, some other kind of fruit. All over the Muslim world fresh *khalal* dates are sold during Ramadan. The prophet also recommended that people break their fast with water, as the body becomes very dehydrated when fasting. Suggestions of foods with which to break the fast are listed below. Furthermore, the food eaten when preparing to fast should be given consideration. A Jewish wisdom tells that extreme and persistent hunger makes the body grow weak and therefore does nothing but distract the mind from God and the point of fasting in the first place is lost. Several sayings of Muhammad recommend that abstainees eat well during the Ramadan hours of sundown. Typically, in the Muslim world, the fast is slowly broken but is followed by feasting which goes on well into the night. However, the body may take several days to readjust to rich foods after a sustained period of fasting. It might therefore be wise to gently awaken the digestive system by slowly re-introducing rich foods into the diet. Food should be eaten even slower than normal and over-eating is best avoided.

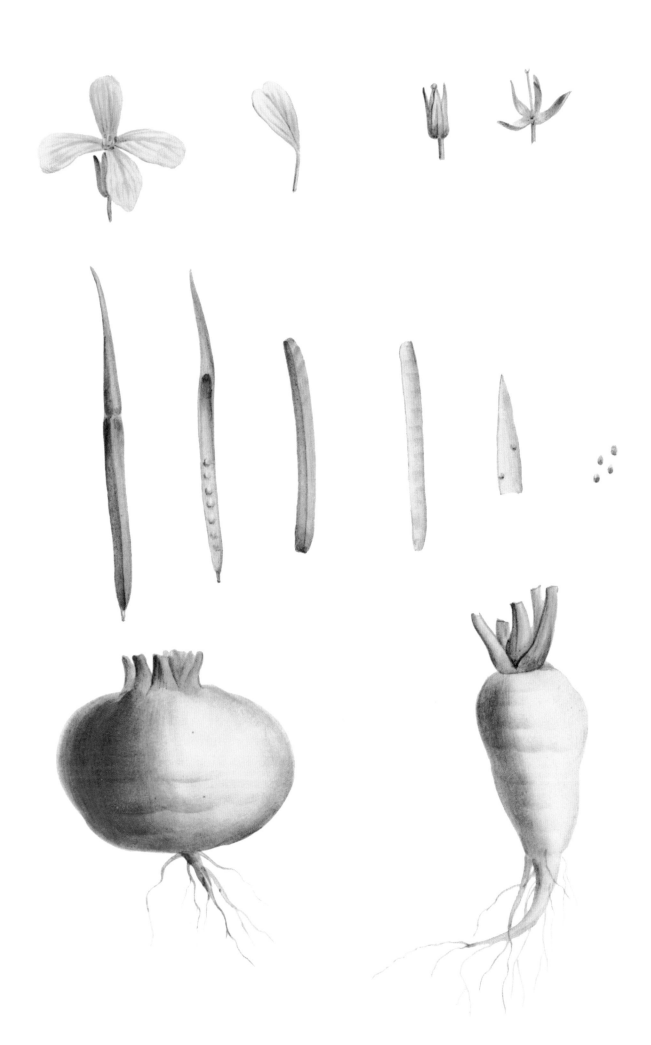

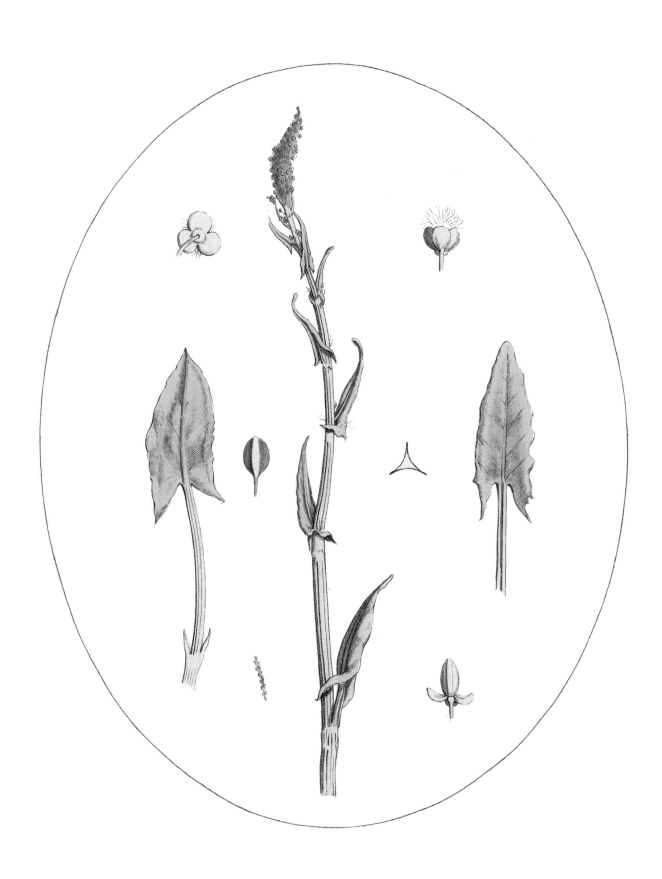

FOODS WITH WHICH TO BREAK THE FAST

Fresh dates, dried dates *if the fresh variety are unobtainable*

Yogurt, *see page* 76

Lentil and vegetable soup *see page* 134

Lentil and zucchini soup *see page* 135

Lentil soup with cumin and onion *see page* 136

Cucumber and yogurt cold soup *see page* 147

Halwa with dates *see page* 303

Smoked date sandwich *see page* 304

Mamoul with dates *see page* 304

Ayran yogurt drink *see page* 331

Small amounts of fresh vegetables

Freshly pressed fruit juice, especially apricot

DIGESTION

'Never have a meal until the one before it has been digested.' IBN SINA

Ensuring that food is properly digested is a crucial part of healthy eating, as it can help to reduce the chances of serious weight-gain or health problems. Muhammad's advice on this matter shows that he appreciated the importance of allowing our bodies to digest food properly. He encouraged people to take small bites, chew well and not reach for more food until they had finished their mouthful. He is reported by As Suyuti to have said, *'Chew your meat well, because then it is more easily digested and more nutritious'* [SAYING OF MUHAMMAD RELATED BY AS SUYUTI]. Modern research has proven that chewing food extensively helps the food to break down, rendering it easier to digest. More than this, however, Muhammad is also reported to have said, *'I do not eat reclining'* [SAYING OF MUHAMMAD RELATED BY AL BUKHARI]. Good posture is also a very important part of ensuring good digestion. Slumping and slouching while eating can, indeed, hinder the food passing smoothly through our bodies and so lead to indigestion. It is also recommended that people take a gentle walk after a late meal.

CLEANLINESS

'After he had washed their feet, had put on his robe, and had returned to the table, he said to them … "If I, your Lord and your Teacher, have washed your feet, you ought to also wash one another's feet."' JOHN 13:6

The story of Jesus washing the feet of the apostles before the Last Supper highlights the importance of cleanliness, especially before meals (although in a modern context, this would apply more to washing your hands). Muhammad also encouraged cleanliness around food and eating. He believed that it was very important to wash before and after meals. Indeed, the Muslim practice of eating only with the right hand shows awareness of hygiene. It makes sense to separate out the functions of the hands, given that in the Muslim world one is assigned to doing ablutions and performing tasks liable to come into contact with germs. Muhammad was also an early advocate of regular oral hygiene. It was related that Hudhaifa said, *'Whenever the Prophet arose at night, he used to clean his teeth with a Siwak'* [SAYINGS AND ACTS OF MUHAMMAD RELATED BY AL BUKHARI]. He is reported to have said that, were it not so difficult to observe, he would have insisted that everybody brushed their teeth with this little reed before each prayer meeting.

PRAYER

'Then Jesus took the loaves, and when he had given thanks, he distributed them to those who were seated.' JOHN 6:11

Prayer around food and meals is a common theme in all three faiths. Jesus gave thanks and blessed food before it was eaten. Indeed, all three religions have traditions which involve prayer preceding a meal. The American feast of Thanksgiving sees a whole nation symbolically thanking God for the bounty of the New World. While the primary function of prayer is to give thanks to God for the food about to be eaten, it is also beneficial to our general health. By praying and taking time out before dining, we can clear our minds and relax, allowing us to take stock of our

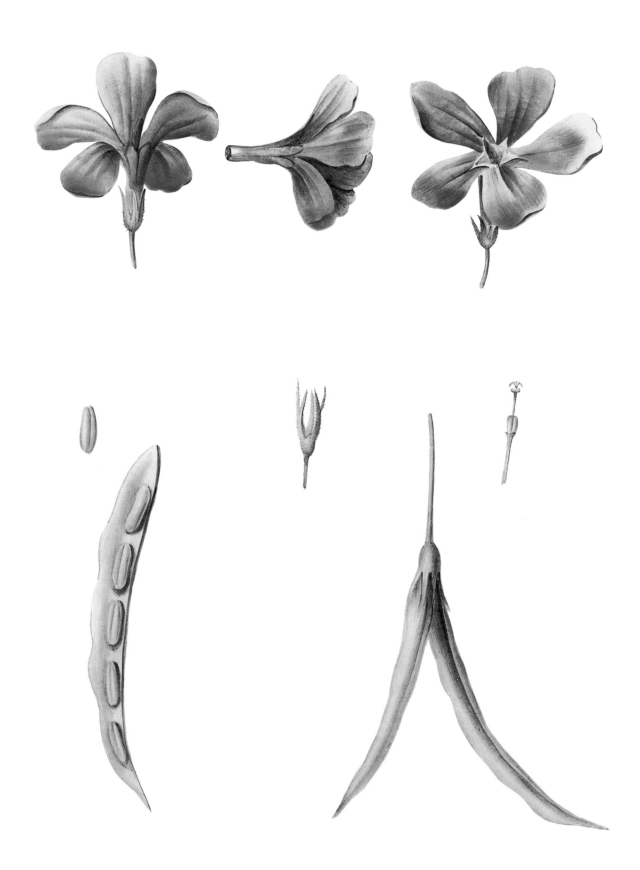

situation and think about the food we are eating. Such reflection before eating helps us to be thankful for the food, think about how much we eat and, hopefully, exercise temperance. In Islam, the poses traditionally adopted for prayer facilitate good posture and encourage us to straighten our bodies, thus helping to smooth digestion. If the whole routine is performed five times a day, it provides a reasonable form of light exercise, stimulating circulation and keeping the body supple.

MODERATION

'Children of Adam, dress well when you attend your mosques. Eat and drink, but avoid excess. He does not love the intemperate.' QURAN, THE HEIGHTS 7:29

Of all the guidelines associated with eating, moderation is perhaps the most important. Hippocrates, the father of medicine, noted that the maintenance of good health depended heavily on refraining from eating and drinking too much. It is through ignoring this most basic principle that there is so much obesity, diabetes, high cholesterol and other diet-related health problems in the Western world. All three faiths attach significant importance to the idea of employing moderation regarding diet and all areas of life. Muhammad spoke about the value of moderation, believing that just as a plant dies from being over-watered, humans will suffer from being over-fed. He seems to have understood how easy it is for man to be tempted to eat more than he needs, and advised that, as a rule of thumb, it is good to remember that 'food for two suffices for three; and food for three suffices for four.' More and more frequently, modern Western portions of food entirely exceed our dietary requirements.

Calorific fast food, which is generally high in saturated fat and low in nutrients and fibre, has come to play an important role in the Western diet. Super-sized portions of these foods far exceed a human's dietary requirements, especially if one has a sedentary lifestyle. According to the religious texts, in order to have a truly healthy diet, we need to listen to our bodies and answer their need: put simply, over-eating is not inspired eating. It is detrimental to our health and gluttony is perceived to be immoral in all three faiths. The principle of eating according to our needs rather than our wants seems to be promoted as a key to maintaining good health: *'Give me neither poverty nor riches; feed me with food convenient for me'* [PROVERBS 30:8]. The best rule of thumb to follow when trying to shed excess weight is to greatly increase vegetable consumption, eat adequate amounts of fruit and lean protein, drink plenty of water and avoid foods with a high carbohydrate or fat content. The recipes listed below facilitate weight loss but are by no means effective unless they are balanced with physical exercise.

All salads with heavily reduced oil or tahina
Ibrahim's fingers *see page* 104
Lentil and vegetable soup *see page* 134
Mushroom and lentil soup *see page* 135
Lentil and zucchini soup *see page* 135
Lentil soup with cumin and onions, grilled *see page* 136
Artichoke soup *see page* 139
Gourd and cinnamon soup *see page* 143
All the vegetable dishes with heavily reduced oil and butter.
Meat and wheat puree *see page* 158
Burghul and vegetables *see page* 162
Burghul and lentils *see page* 162
Millet and vegetable porridge *see page* 163
Perfumed saffron rice *see page* 172
Rice with spinach *see page* 172
Grilled or barbecued lean meat with spice rub
St. Peter's fish *see page* 208
Any grilled fish
Galilee grilled sardines *see page* 208
Rock salt fish *see page* 223
Fish with capers *see page* 226
Rock salt chicken *see page* 245
Chicken with green wheat *see page* 248

VEGETARIANISM

Throughout the spiritual texts, people are warned to eat meat with temperance and restraint. In Genesis, meat is only really allowed following the flood and even then reluctantly so. It would seem that red meat was not consumed in the Garden of Eden. Although vegetarianism as a movement emerged in the nineteenth century, there have been conscientious individuals and groups who have abstained from eating meat and animal produce throughout history. In the classical world, Pythagoras, Plutarch and Ovid were among those who abstained from eating flesh for both physical and moral reasons. Although the three faiths take the orthodox view that man, as master of his environment, has the right to consume animals, they have known many pious abstentious figures through the ages, such as monks and sufis. A number of recipes in this book are suggested as being particularly suitable for vegetarians. There are many more that contain no meat, but these dishes do contain non-animal protein sources and can therefore be served as part of a balanced vegetarian meal. Today there are many types of vegetarians: ovo-lacto vegetarians who eat eggs and dairy products, vegans who abstain from consuming all animal produce, and pescetarians who abstain from meat and poultry but eat fish. These recipes have been selected for those vegetarians that eat dairy and eggs and therefore are not necessarily suitable for vegans. Although there are many recipes in this book that do not contain meat, the following suggestions are designed to help the vegetarian select balanced meals from this collection.

Jerusalem siege bread *see page* 57
Fatah with chickpeas and olive oil *see page* 62
Hummus fatah *see page* 62
Zahid's onion and pomegranate bread pudding *see page* 65
Fava bean and lemon salad *see page* 119
Fava bean and coriander salad *see page* 121
Chickpea salad *see page* 122
Chickpea and tahina salad *see page* 122
Hummus with sesame *see page* 125

Lentil and vegetable soup *see page* 134
Lentil and bean stew *see page* 135
Lentil and zucchini soup *see page* 135
Mushroom and lentil soup *see page* 135
Lentil soup with cumin and onions *see page* 136
Burghul and lentils *see page* 162
Rice and lentils *see page* 172
Vegetarian stuffing *see page* 186
Swindler's kibbeh *see page* 292

FEASTING

Feasts were highly important events in the Holy Land as, for many, they broke the monotony of an otherwise mundane farming existence. For the Hebrews, feasts marked turning points in the history of their faith and remembrance of their salvation. Feasts brought ancient communities together and were characterised by singing, dancing, offerings and processions. They often involved a sacrifice to the Lord. The three principal feasts in the Hebrew calendar were Passover, Pentecost and the Feast of the Tabernacles. In the Byzantine period the calendar of the early Christian Church began to emerge, with the most important feast being Easter, the resurrection. The following recipes are often enjoyed at feasts and celebrations.

Maklouba *see page* 173
Stuffed calabash gourd *see page* 183
Stuffed gourd Aleppo style *see page* 184
Stuffed pomegranate zucchini *see page* 186
Stuffed aubergine *see page* 190
Fish in paradise sauce *see page* 228
Barbecued leg of lamb *see page* 272
Prophet's tharid *see page* 281

QUICK DISHES SUITABLE FOR CHILDREN

The most important principles when feeding children are nutritional balance and fresh ingredients. It is unusual for children to appreciate heavily spiced or perfumed food. In general children can eat adult dishes, with smaller, more manageable portions, mashed or liquidised for babies and toddlers. The following recipes have been selected as they are quick and simple to prepare, nutritious and easy for children to digest.

Fatah with chickpeas and olive oil *see page* 62
Hummus Fatah *see page* 62
Fatah with chicken *see page* 63
Yogurt *see page* 76
Northern Moutabal *see page* 106
Caviar of aubergines *see page* 106
Pomegranate Batersch *see page* 107
Hummus *see page* 125 *(use cooked chickpeas)*
Wheat and vegetable soup *see page* 142
Chicken and rice soup *see page* 142
Yogurt soup *see page* 147
Labaneyeh *see page* 148
Meat and wheat puree *see page* 158
Burghul with raisins and pine nuts *see page* 161
Pomegranate and walnut burghul *see page* 161
Burghul and vegetables *see page* 162
Millet and vegetable porridge *see page* 163
Rice with herbs *see page* 167
Rice with pine nuts and raisins *see page* 168
Rice with dates *see page* 168
Saffron rice *see page* 171
Rice with spinach *see page* 172
Rice with gourd *see page* 173

Jonah's gourd mash *see page* 183
Gourd and sesame mash *see page* 183
Zucchini mash *see page* 187
Zucchini gratin *see page* 187
Mallow with fruit and nuts *see page* 191
Spinach with walnuts and pomegranate *see page* 192
Creation spinach *see page* 192
Leek casserole *see page* 199
Sweet Apollonian fish *see page* 222
Rice with fish *see page* 227
Moses sole *see page* 228
Chicken and burghul *see page* 247
Chicken and rice *see page* 248
Kibbeh paste – all kibbeh recipes *see page* 284

HUNTING

'Isaac loved Jacob because he was fond of game; but Rebekah loved Ezekiel.' GENESIS 25:28

Hunting was not a widespread activity in the Holy Land. It was reserved for times of severe hunger. However, there were some hunters of note in the Bible, such as Jacob, son of Isaac. Deer, wild goat and partridge did make their way to the tables of kings and the wealthy and so we may conclude that there was some hunting activity. It must be noted, however, that as dietary laws developed, many Jews would not eat game unless it had been killed in the ritual sacrificial manner. Birds such as falcons, vultures, buzzards, kites and crows were hunted by the Egyptians, especially the upper classes, as a pastime. It is interesting to note that such birds were forbidden to Moses and the children of Israel soon after their departure from Egypt.

GAZELLE

'Solomon's provision for one day was thirty cors of fine flour, and sixty cors of meal ... besides harts, gazelles, roebucks and fatted fowl.' I KINGS 4:22–23

Although deer itself is not mentioned in the Bible, there are several references to gazelle. Gazelle is similar to a small antelope, roe or roebuck. It is graceful and swift of foot. Ashael is compared to a swift-footed wild gazelle in the book of Samuel [II SAMUEL 2:19]. It is deemed 'clean' according to Mosaic Law, and furthermore it is said that Solomon's commissary kept a good stock of gazelle in the royal larder, alongside hart and roebuck [I KINGS 4:23]. Deer being the closest relative of these animals eaten today, it seems reasonable to include it as a type of meat in this book. In fact, venison is one of the leanest, and therefore healthiest, red meats available today. Not only is it a good source of B vitamins, protein and iron, it is exceptionally low in fat and cholesterol.

ROAST VENISON

1 venison haunch
5 garlic cloves, sliced
125ml (½ cup) olive oil
4 onions, sliced
4 bay leaves
1 tablespoon pepper corns
1 teaspoon cloves
2 tablespoons thyme
1 tablespoon marjoram
1 tablespoon salt
60g (4 tablespoons) honey
1 litre (4 cups) wine vinegar
1 litre (4 cups) apple juice

1. Wash the meat and pierce in several places and insert the garlic slices.
2. Combine the marinade ingredients. Place the meat in a large dish, cover with the marinade and leave in a cool place for 24 hours. Turn the meat in the marinade at regular intervals.
3. Place the meat in a pre-heated oven at 160C (325F) and cook for 2½ to 3 hours, basting regularly. Serve hot.

THE SPIRITUAL
BALANCE

Humanity is a light conceived by the host
The guide who found us when we were lost,
The truth of this order, the way of the earth
Maligned and abused from the dawn of its birth,
And man's inner thoughts in all of their forms
Emitted a wave of spiritual storms,
The way of Godly food divine
The way to health, obey the sign,
Measured by manna from heaven came
To immune the heart, to soothe the lame,
From Quran, Bible and Hebrew scroll
Drawn from strength to sustain us all,
The ancient, sage and the pillars of right
Shall evil drive from your path and sight,
If mind and body are nourished well
Spirit and life inside will dwell,
Your earthly body shall at last be sent
To leave at death a soul content.

S. D'ANTIOC

Site of Ezion-Geber, Gulf of Akaba   David Roberts

INDEX

A
Abraham, 21
Almond, 241
  chicken with, 241
ancient table, 24
Antioch table spice, 35
appetizers, 85
  (*see* simple and side)
apple, 315
apricot, 247(*see* plum)
  meat with 272
  kibbeh in sauce, 293
artichoke, 108
  with olive oil, 108
  salad, 108
  soup, 139
  and lamb stew, 139
asparagus, 197
  with meat, 197
  with meat, 275
aubergine, 189
  fatah with, 64
  northern moutabel, 106
  caviar of aubergine, 106
  pomegranate batersch, 107
  slices with yogurt, 189
  with yogurt, 189
  stuffed, 190
  and zucchini moussaka, 190
  makloupa, 173

B
baking, 55
basil, 88
barbecue and grilling, 268
barley, 61
  loaves, 61
bay leaf, 280

bean, 117
  fava salad, 117
  fava and lemon salad, 119
  fava and coriander salad and lentil
    soup, 135
beef, 285
  Emessa stew, 285
beetroot, 100
  yogurt and parsley, 100
  with yogurt and mint, 100
  and sesame salad, 101
beverages, 323
  mint infusion, 327
  liquorice infusion, 328
  liquorice water, 328
  ginger infusion, 330
  maizena, 331
  khfafe, 331
  sahleb, 331
  Ayran yogurt drink, 331
breakfast
  safiha, 65
BIBLE
  Genesis 1:29–30, 177
  Genesis 9:3, 265
  Genesis 9:4, 268
  Genesis 25:34, 129
  Genesis 40:9–11, 105
  Genesis 43:11, 311
  Exodus 12:8–9, 272
  Leviticus 2:13, 34
  Leviticus 10:9, 325
  Leviticus 11:9, 205
  Leviticus 11:13, 237
  Numbers 9:11, 87
  Numbers 11:5, 205
  Numbers 11:7, 121
  Numbers 11:31, 256

Deuteronomy 8:7–9, 60
Deuteronomy 14:20, 237
Deuteronomy 24:6, 54
Deuteronomy 32:13–14, 73
Judges 6:19, 287
Ruth 2:14, 41
I Samuel 8:13, 297
II Samuel 5:23, 312
II Samuel 17:27–28, 117
Job 30:4, 191
Proverbs 15:17, 179
Proverbs 30:33, 74
Song of Solomon 6:11, 308
Isaiah 1:8, 97
Isaiah 28:24–25, 136
Isaiah 28:25, 58
Isaiah 28:27, 231
Isaiah 41:19, 307
Isaiah 43:24, 316
Ezekiel 4:9, 55, 163
Jonah 1:17, 207
Jonah 4:6, 183
Matthew 4:4, 337
Matthew 4:19, 218
Matthew 5:6, 7, 340
Matthew 5:13, 34
Matthew 13:31, 43
Matthew 23:23, 329
Matthew 23:37, 239
Luke 11:3, 53
Luke 11:42, 29
Luke 15:22–23, 282
Luke 24:42, 205, 208
John 4:14, 323
John 6:11, 344
John 6:13, 61
John 6:48, 51
John 13:6, 344
John 29:9–10, 208
Colossians 4:15, 209
Revelations 6:13, 301

Revelations 7:17, 271
bread, 51
    khoubiz flat, 56
    Jerusalem siege, 57
    whole flat, 58
    unleavened, 59
    barley loaves, 61
    soaked flat, 62 (see also fatah)
    open faced, 65 (see also safiha)
bitter herbs and salads, 87
    salad of bitter greens, 87
burghul, 161
    and marjoram stew, 141
    and chicken, 247
    lamb with, 278
    with raisins and pine nuts, 161
    pomegranate and walnut, 161
butter, 75
    clarified, 74

C
calf, 282 (see also veal)
caper, 226
    fish with, 226
    skate in browned butter, 226
carob, 318
    cake, 318
citrus fruit, 39
    citron, 39
    lemon, 39
    orange, 39
citrus dressing, 39
chard, 191
    stuffed, 194
    with onion, 194
    spiced stalks, 195
cheese, 78
    Arab jibin, 78
    mizithra, 79
    feta and cucumber salad, 97
    feta, melon and date salad, 98

goat's cheese and cucumber salad, 97
chicken, 239
    fatah with, 63
    and rice soup, 142
    and chickpea soup, 142
    with almonds, 241
    lemon, 242
    with melokhia, 242
    and quince, 243
    Iranian roast, 244
    Syrian stuffed, 244
    rock salt, 245
    slow-cooked with chickpeas, 245
    with plums, 247
    and green wheat, 248
    and rice, 248
    and burghul, 247
chickpea, 122
    fatah with olive oil and, 62
    hummus fatah, 62
    salad, 122
    and tahina salad hummus with
        cumin,125
    hummus bi tahina, 125
    and chicken soup, 142
    slow-cooked chicken with , 245
children, 351
    suggested dishes, 351
cleanliness, 344
cooking methods, 24
coriander, 121
    and fava salad, 121
cucumber, 93
    salad, 93
    and lettuce salad, 97
    and feta, 97
    and goat's cheese salad, 97
    and radish salad, 103
    and yogurt cold soup, 147
cumin, 136
    mushrooms with, 112

hummus with, 125
    lentil soup with onions and, 136

D
dairy, 71
date, 303
    Khalid's fish with, 212
    halwa with, 303
    smoked sandwich, 304
    mamoul, 304
    rice with, 168
dessert, 297
digestion, 343
dill, 232
    Roman mullet, 231
duck, 250
    honeyed, 250
    with olives, 250
    with peaches, 253
    pomegranate roast, 253

E
endive, 92
    salad, 92

F
fasting, 338
    foods with which to break the fast, 343
feasting, 350
    suggested foods, 350
fatah, 62
    bread pudding, 65
    hummus, 62
    with aubergines, 64
    with chick peas and olive oil, 62
    with chicken, 63
    Zahid's onion and pomegranate bread
        pudding, 65
fava bean, 117 (see bean)
fig, 301
    Cakes, 301